The National Gallery
LONDON

New Edition

MICHAEL WILSON

Deputy Keeper at the Gallery

 Letts**Guides**

Charles Letts and Company Limited

© 1982 Philip Wilson Publishers Ltd and Summerfield Press Ltd,
Russell Chambers, Covent Garden, London WC2E 8AA

First edition published in 1978 by
Charles Letts and Company Limited,
Diary House, Borough Road, London SEI IDW

First edition designed by Paul Sharp
New edition designed by Richard Johnson
Edited by Philip Wilson Publishers Ltd
Series Editor: Judy Spours

Produced by Scala Istituto Fotografico Editoriale
Phototypeset by Tradespools Limited, Frome, Somerset

ISBN 0 85667 156 8

Printed in Italy by Arti Grafiche Alinari Baglioni S.p.A., Firenze 1986

Front cover: *Portrait of a Man* (detail) by Titian

Back cover: *The beach at Trouville* (detail) by Monet

The publishers would like to thank the National Gallery for
supplying the colour transparencies, and Angelo Hornak for
doing additional photography including the front cover.

Contents

4   Main dates in the history of the Gallery

5   Introduction

11   Early Italian schools

29   Early northern schools

45   Sixteenth-century Italy

61   Seventeenth-century Holland and Flanders

85   Seventeenth-century Italy, France and Spain

103   The eighteenth century

123   The nineteenth century and after

143   Index

The Gallery is open from 10 am to 6 pm from
Monday to Saturday, and from 2 pm to 6 pm on Sundays.
Admission free.

All dimensions are given in centimetres.

Main dates in the history of the Gallery

1824 foundation of the National Gallery, based on the collection of John Julius Angerstein and displayed in his house at 100 Pall Mall

1828 Sir George Beaumont Gift

1831 Reverend Holwell Carr Bequest

1834 collection moved to 105 Pall Mall

1838 new building opened in Trafalgar Square, designed by Sir William Wilkins

1846 public outcry against the Gallery administration, particularly its cleaning policy

1847 Vernon Gift

1853 Government Select Committee set up to examine the Gallery's constitution

1854 purchase of Krüger Collection

1855 Sir Charles Eastlake, first Director of the Gallery

1856 Turner Bequest

1863 presentation by Queen Victoria, at the wish of Prince Albert, of German paintings from his own collection

1866 Sir William Boxall succeeds as second Director

1871 purchase of seventy-seven paintings from the Peel Collection

1874 Sir Frederick Burton, third Director

1876 Wynn Ellis Bequest
   new wing opened, designed by Edward Barry (rooms 32–40)

1887 the central rooms opened, designed by Sir John Taylor (rooms 13, 29, 31, 39)

1894 Sir Edward Poynter, fourth Director

1897 Tate Gallery first opened, as an annexe to the Gallery

1903 foundation of the National Art-Collections Fund

1906 Sir Charles Holroyd, fifth Director

1910 Salting Bequest

1911 five west rooms opened (rooms 5, 10, 11, 12, 14)

1916 Layard Bequest
   Sir Charles Holmes, sixth Director

1917 Lane Bequest

1923 Samuel Courtauld Fund

1924 Mond Bequest

1929 Sir Augustus Daniel, seventh Director

1934 Sir Kenneth Clark, eighth Director

1939– pictures evacuated to a quarry in Wales, musical recitals held in Gallery building
1945

1945 Sir Philip Hendy, ninth Director

1955 Tate becomes an independent gallery

1968 Sir Martin Davies, tenth Director

1972 Alexander Gift

1973 Sir Michael Levey, eleventh Director

1975 northern extension opened (rooms 16–27)

Introduction

The National Gallery from 1824 to 1981

Viewed from Trafalgar Square, the National Gallery with its dome, turrets and portico presents an aspect which is both severe and dignified. The Gallery had been established for fourteen years when, on April 9th 1838, it first opened in this newly-completed building. With its neo-Palladian grandeur, the façade, which remains virtually unchanged, gives some idea of the respect and seriousness with which the concept of a national collection was then regarded.

This had not always been the case. At the end of the eighteenth century, when a national gallery was first being seriously considered, the government showed little interest. Some, like John Constable, were actually opposed to the idea. In 1823, by which date national galleries had already been established in Vienna, Paris, Amsterdam, Madrid and Berlin, the government failed to respond to Sir George Beaumont's offer to give his famous collection to the nation as soon as proper accommodation could be provided. However, in 1824, when it was discovered that the collection of John Julius Angerstein, a Russian-born financier recently deceased, was on offer to the Prince of Orange for £70,000, the government was finally spurred into action. Probably influenced by Sir George Beaumont's promise, and a similar offer by the Reverend Holwell Carr, the House of Commons voted £60,000 for the purchase, preservation and exhibition of the Angerstein pictures. Thirty-eight were bought, among them fine works by Claude, Rubens and Rembrandt, together with the lease of Angerstein's house.

It was there, at 100 Pall Mall, in premises never intended for public display, that the growing collection remained for ten years. The Angerstein pictures were joined by those of Beaumont and Holwell Carr while others were contributed by the Treasury. A purpose-built structure was urgently needed and in 1831 designs submitted by William Wilkins for a new gallery were approved. Two years later work began on the site made vacant by the demolition of the King's mews on the north side of Trafalgar Square. However, early in 1834 it was discovered that Angerstein's house was in danger of collapse and the Gallery had

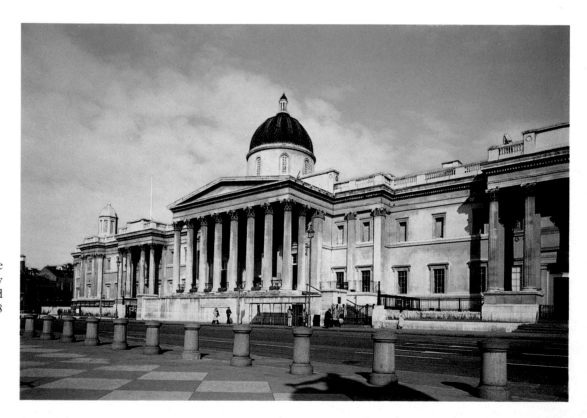

The main façade of the Gallery, designed by William Wilkins and built 1834–8

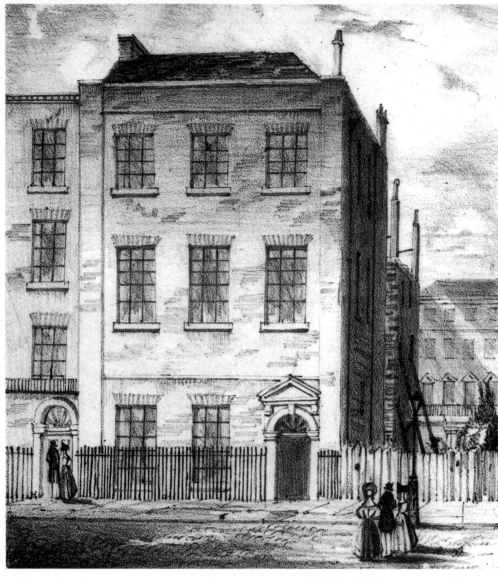

The Gallery's first home at 100 Pall Mall, Julius Angerstein's former house

to be removed to even more cramped quarters at 105 Pall Mall. There it was obliged to remain until Wilkins' building was ready.

In fact, when it was ready, the new gallery offered little more than an imposing façade. It may have improved the Gallery's prestige, but it was insufficient to accommodate a rapidly expanding collection. The site was unusually long and narrow. Consequently Wilkins' building comprised only one range of top-lit exhibition rooms with living quarters for the Keeper and offices beneath. Furthermore, until 1869 the section to the east of the dome was occupied by the Royal Academy.

Although the problems of lack of space, poor ventilation, dirt and noise continued to trouble the Trustees, a crisis arose after the move to Trafalgar Square that was to have far greater consequences. Late in 1846 when a group of newly-cleaned pictures was exhibited, a storm of protest was levelled against the administrtion of the Collection and its policy of cleaning. It was claimed that such pictures as Rubens' '*Peace and War*' (p 78) and Titian's *Bacchus and Ariadne* (p 56) had been destroyed. They are with us today still in good condition, but in the mid-nineteenth century the public was accustomed to seeing pictures obscured by layers of dirt and discoloured varnish, the 'tone' of an old master. When the outcry was renewed in 1853, a Select Committee was set up by the government to examine the situation, and as a result of its Report the Gallery's constitution was revised.

A Keeper had been appointed in 1824 and later a 'committee of six gentlemen', including Sir George Beaumont and the painter Sir Thomas Lawrence, had been nominated to supervise the Collection, but no regular meetings were held and recommendations for the purchase of pictures were made to the Treasury very much according to the whim of

6

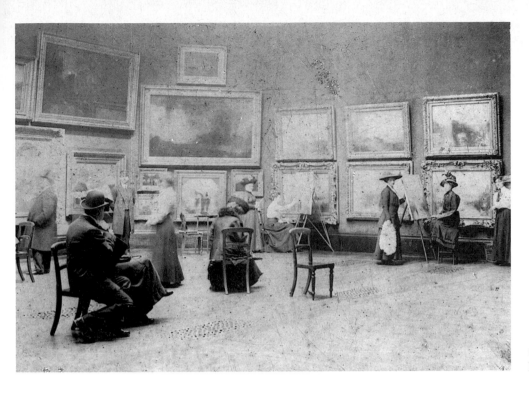

Copyists at work in the Turner Room, 1907

individuals. In 1855, as a result of the inquiry of 1853, the first Director, Sir Charles Lock Eastlake, was appointed and an annual purchase grant was allocated. The responsibility for the purchase of pictures now rested with him alone, and while preference had previously been given to pictures by acknowledged masters of the sixteenth and seventeenth centuries, it was now resolved to build the Collection on historical principles and to include works by the precursors of these celebrated artists, the 'primitives' of the fourteenth and fifteenth centuries.

Thus, during the second half of the century a systematic policy led to the acquisition of many of the Gallery's greatest treasures. A number of considerable gifts and bequests also swelled the Collection. The Vernon Gift of 1847 and the Turner bequest of 1856 contributed many modern British works, most of which, until the opening of Edward Barry's new wing in 1876, were housed elsewhere. The purchase of seventy-seven pictures in 1871 from the Peel Collection and the Wynn Ellis bequest of 1876 suddenly gave the Gallery an extensive representation of Dutch painting, but once again necessitated an expansion to the building. Barry's rooms in the east of the building were therefore followed in 1887 by a central spine of rooms and a new vestibule designed by Sir John Taylor. The five rooms to the west that balance Barry's wing were finally completed in 1911, after the buildings adjacent to the Gallery had been deemed a fire hazard and demolished.

Meanwhile, all but a small selection of the British pictures had left Trafalgar Square for the new national gallery at Millbank, opened in 1897, where they remain today. The Tate Gallery, as it is known, was made an independent museum in 1955 and also became the home of the national collection of modern painting and sculpture. Space was thereby gained for new foreign acquisitions, and with the Salting and Lane bequests of 1910 and 1917 came the first considerable group of nineteenth-century French paintings.

With the retirement of the third Director, Sir Frederick Burton, in 1894 there came another significant change for the Gallery. A revision of the constitution placed the authority for the purchase of pictures once again with the Trustees, and while it was hoped that unwise or erratic purchases would thereby be avoided, an era was thus terminated during which men of exceptional ability had been able to exercise their flair and talent unhindered in securing top-rate pictures.

However, by the beginning of the twentieth century the circumstances in which Eastlake had operated had greatly changed. The Gallery now had formidable competitors, particularly in America, and if acquisitions this century have often been less spectacular than formerly, they have also been more difficult and more expensive. The declining fortunes of

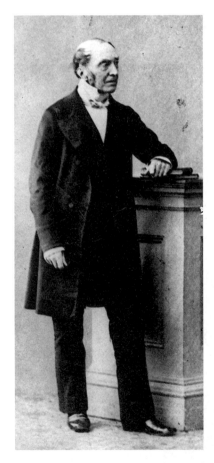

Sir Charles Lock Eastlake (1793–1865), first Director of the Gallery from 1855 to 1865

the country have been reflected in the infrequency of major gifts or bequests. The present century has witnessed the sale of many English collections, and, with the absence of wealthy buyers in this country, a steady stream of old master works to Europe, the U.S.A., and latterly Japan and the Middle East.

Increased demand and a dwindling stock of masterpieces has caused art prices to soar, with individual paintings now commonly fetching in excess of £1 million at auction. The Gallery lacks the funds to stem altogether the export flow at such prices, and provincial museums are even more poorly placed. Nevertheless, the Gallery now has a substantial annual grant from the Government which continues to enable the occasional purchase of outstanding works, which otherwise would almost certainly leave the country. Pictures like Rembrandt's portrait of *Hendrickje Stoffels* (p 67) and Altdorfer's altarpiece, *Christ taking leave of His Mother* (p 43) have been bought, and, in 1981, Claude's *The enchanted castle*, a poetic late landscape admired by Keats, Hazlitt and Ruskin, was purchased.

In making such acquisitions the Gallery has been generously supported by the National Art-Collections Fund, and since its foundation by the National Heritage Memorial Fund. When a sale is by private treaty the Gallery is able also to negotiate a very favourable price which benefits the vendor too, since no tax is payable. This applies only, of course, when the owner is domiciled in Great Britain, and otherwise the Gallery competes in a world market. In 1978 it bid successfully in New York for *The Winnower* by Jean-François Millet (p 131). Perhaps its greatest coup of recent years was the purchase at auction in 1980 of Rubens' magnificent early oil painting on panel of *Samson and Delilah* (p 79) for £2 million.

In times of such astronomical prices gifts and bequests are particularly valuable – if rarer than in the past. The Gallery has been fortunate to add to its collection as recent bequests a still life by Kalf (p 77), a landscape by Cézanne, and Monet's outstanding painting of *Bathers at La Grenouillère* (p 132).

The Gallery's acquisitions are much determined by circumstance. It always aims to buy paintings of the highest quality, but cannot predict what will become available. Nevertheless, an effort has been made in recent years to purchase in some of those areas previously neglected – particularly the French eighteenth century and the nineteenth century. Many of the pictures illustrated in the last two sections of this book have been purchased in the last decade, and some, such as those by Fragonard, 'Le Douanier' Rousseau, Klimt, Moreau, Redon, Matisse and Picasso, are by artists who were not previously represented, and whose work is very rare in this country. Such acquisitions have the merit not only of extending the historical representation of the Collection, but also of broadening its scope, demonstrating the limitless diversity of inspiration to be found in European painting.

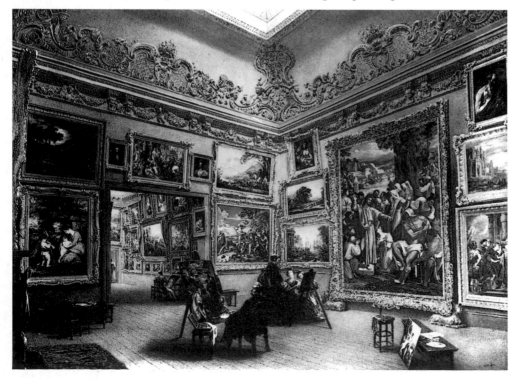

The interior of the National Gallery at 100 Pall Mall in a watercolour by Frederick MacKenzie (Victoria and Albert Museum)

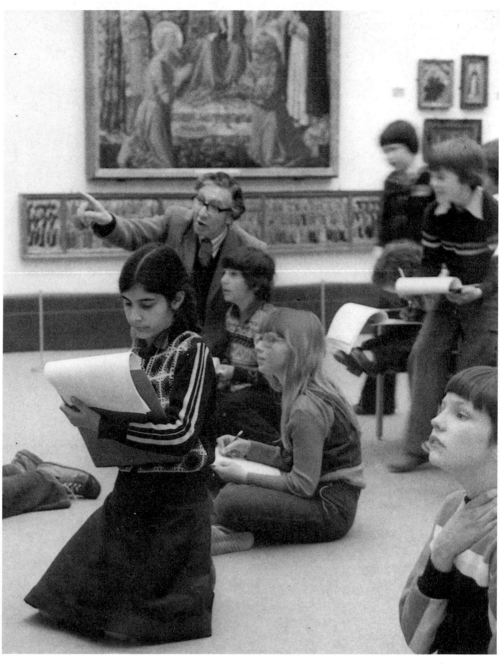

Children engaged in a Gallery quiz

As the range of the Collection has been extended, so an attempt has been made to give all pictures the space and surroundings they need if each is to be seen and appreciated in its own right, and not merely as a museum piece. The opening of the northern extension in 1975 provided thirteen new galleries and, although further expansion will be required, has temporarily alleviated the problem of space. These rooms are equipped with modern lighting and climate controls to protect the paintings on display there, especially those on wood, which require stable environmental conditions, and a programme has begun to extend air-conditioning throughout the old building to provide similar protection to the whole Collection.

Today's National Gallery is not the creature it was. A visitor from the nineteenth century might be excused for not recognising it. Gone is the atmosphere of reverence and sanctity, and the building bustles with visitors of all kinds: tourists, children, scholars and native Londoners. There are many more pictures to be enjoyed, and thanks to a programme of several decades of restoration by the Gallery's Conservation Department, they are in good order and clearly visible; with the dirt of centuries removed they are as close to their original appearance as possible. While the restorers repair the damage of time, the Scientific Department conducts research into the deterioration of pictures in order that preventive

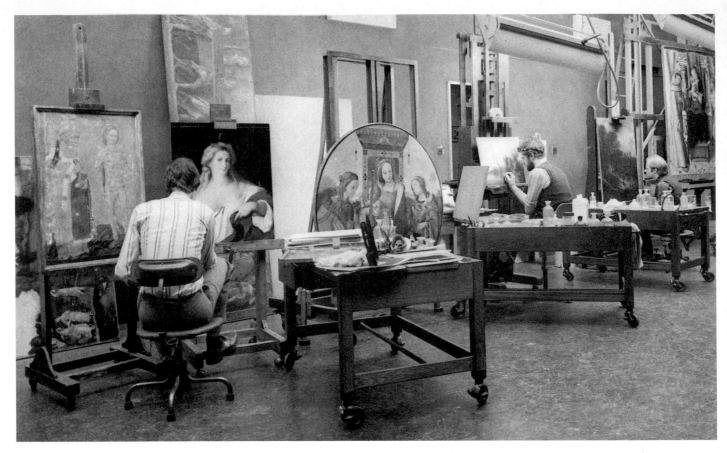

measures can be introduced. Information on the paintings is available to the public in every room, a shop sells books, reproductions, postcards and slides, and there is a constantly changing programme of exhibitions, quizzes, children's activities and audio-visual shows to help to generate enthusiasm for, and understanding of, the treasures the Gallery contains.

The role of the Gallery has thus changed dramatically. It continues, as it has always done, to acquire, preserve and display masterpieces of painting. But it is finding means as never before to show works to their best advantage, and to make them accessible to a modern audience. Education has become a major part of the Gallery's function, and an Education Department now exists to serve the needs of schools, students and the adult visitor. Education in a picture gallery consists of much more than imparting information about history, dates and technical data. It depends rather upon stimulating a response, opening the eyes of visitors to the vast range of visual delights that painting holds in store, and engendering for now and future generations a true sense of the value of the exceptional work of art. It is this that the National Gallery aims to do.

Restorers at work in the Conservation Department

Early Italian schools

The first early Italian works to be acquired by the National Gallery were Lorenzo Monaco's two groups of saints presented, not purchased, in 1848, twenty-four years after the founding of the Gallery. Now the altarpiece can be seen complete with its centre panel showing *The Coronation of the Virgin* (p 14) which was later purchased by the Gallery in 1902.

For the first thirty years of the Gallery's existence until its reconstitution in 1855, the Keeper and Trustees had pursued a conservative and narrow policy of acquisition, inherited from the great private collectors of the eighteenth century. The pictures in the Angerstein, Beaumont and Holwell Carr collections which formed the nucleus of the new Gallery were for the most part by the accepted masters of the sixteenth and seventeenth centuries, and in the early years of the Gallery's history it was predominantly Italian paintings from this period that were acquired, works by artists such as Correggio, Titian, Annibale Carracci, and Guido Reni. Sir Robert Peel, a Trustee from 1827 until his death in 1850, regarded early Italian pictures merely as curiosities and opposed their purchase, an attitude which reflected the general feeling.

When, in 1846, a scandal broke over the Gallery's cleaning of its pictures, criticism was also directed against the purchasing policy of the Trustees, in particular against their predilection for the artists of the Bolognese School, such as Guido Reni. His *Susanna and the Elders* purchased in 1845 was described by Ruskin as 'devoid alike of art and decency'. Ruskin pursued his point in a letter to *The Times* in January 1847 in which he attacked 'the cumbering of our walls with pictures that have no single virtue, no colour, no drawing, no character, no history, no thought' and the failure to acquire any works by such artists as Perugino, Fra Angelico, Fra Bartolommeo and Verrocchio, artists who he thought interpreted nature with greater sincerity and purity of sentiment.

Consequently, when the Inquiry of 1853 was set up to investigate the affairs of the Gallery, it did not fail to report upon the purchasing policy. The Treasury Minute of 1855 which abolished the old Gallery constitution also advised with respect to purchases that 'preference should be given to good specimens of the Italian schools, including those of the earliest masters'. The new Director, Sir Charles Lock Eastlake, whose own tastes accorded with this new policy, began at once to put it into effect. It is largely due to Eastlake's initiative and energy that the Gallery has such a magnificent collection of fifteenth and sixteenth century Italian paintings. He had already served as Keeper, and now as Director he was able to exercise fully his powers of discrimination. Throughout the course of his directorship he undertook regular tours of Italy to acquire suitable paintings for the Collection, and it was in Italy that he was taken ill and died in the winter of 1865.

From his first visit in 1855 he returned with, among other fine things, a Botticelli, a Bellini and Mantegna's *Virgin and Child* (p 20). The following year he purchased the triptych by Perugino (p 28) and the marvellous St Sebastian altarpiece by the brothers Pollaiuolo (p 19). Towards the end of 1857 he purchased in Italy twenty-two works from the Lombardi Baldi collection, including *The Battle of San Romano* (p 17), one of three paintings executed by Uccello around 1450 for the Medici Palace in Florence. The next year saw the purchase of works by Cossa, Cima, Crivelli, and a fine late painting by Giovanni Bellini, *The Madonna of the meadow* (p 25), and in 1861 the prize acquisition was *The Baptism of Christ* (p 22) by Piero della Francesca, an artist then barely recognised, purchased at the Uzielli sale for only £241. Eastlake's love of early Italian painting was inherited by his successors, Sir William Boxall and Sir Frederick Burton, and the prodigious stream of pictures acquired during the second half of the nineteenth century changed the whole balance of the Collection.

Among them were early fourteenth-century works by the first great painter of the Sienese School, Duccio. *The Annunciation* (p 13) is one of three panels in the Gallery from the *Maestà* altarpiece which was executed for Siena Cathedral between 1308/11. The majority of the early Italian works in the Collection are religious in subject and were commissioned for churches. In the fifteenth century there was a dramatic move away from the conventions of Sienese painting towards a more naturalistic and monumental approach. The Madonna (p 16) in the panel by Masaccio, an artist working in Florence at the beginning of the century, is no longer flat and stylised: the pattern of light and shade gives an illusion of depth. Later still, in the St Sebastian altarpiece (p 19) by the brothers Pollaiuolo, the traditional gold background has disappeared and the figures are shown in a variety of contrasting poses. The study of anatomy and perspective enabled painting to become more realistic and dramatic. The revival of interest in the art of antiquity led to an enthusiasm for profile portraits (p 19) in imitation of Roman coins and medals, and for subjects drawn from classical mythology, for example Botticelli's *Venus and Mars* (p 27) and the strange scene showing a satyr lamenting a dead nymph by Piero di Cosimo (p 28).

However, these early Italian works were still not regarded as masterpieces in their own right. In the Report of 1853 the Select Committee had drawn the following analogy: 'What Chaucer and Spenser are to Shakespeare and Milton, Giotto and Masaccio are to the great masterpieces of the Florentine School.' There was little doubt for Eastlake that the peak of western painting had been reached in Italy at the beginning of the sixteenth century. The early Italian pictures he collected were of importance in that they illustrated the early stages in the development of painting, and the art of the late sixteenth and seventeenth century demonstrated the decline.

Today it is possible to regard these pictures as independent achievements, different from but not necessarily inferior to the painting of the High Renaissance. In fact, there are surprising affinities between the early 'primitive' Italian works and twentieth-century painting, especially in the semi-abstract flattening of the picture plane, which no doubt make it easier for a modern audience to respond to these paintings than it was for our nineteenth-century predecesors, who were accustomed to a modern art that was much more naturalistic.

As they are different, so these pictures require an appropriate means of display. In recent years the Gallery has attempted to provide more sympathetic surroundings for its early collection, hanging them on plaster-lined walls, for example, in tiled rooms. Many of the elaborate and fanciful Victorian frames have been removed, and when works exist only in fragmentary form, either gravely damaged or as part of a polyptych, an attempt is made to show them as such and not, misleadingly, as intact, framed, easel-paintings. The fragments of Perugino's altarpiece (p 28), for example, had been enlarged in the last century to give the impression of a completely intact triptych. During recent cleaning all the nineteenth-century extensions to the panels were removed so that, except for minor restoration, all that now remains is original work.

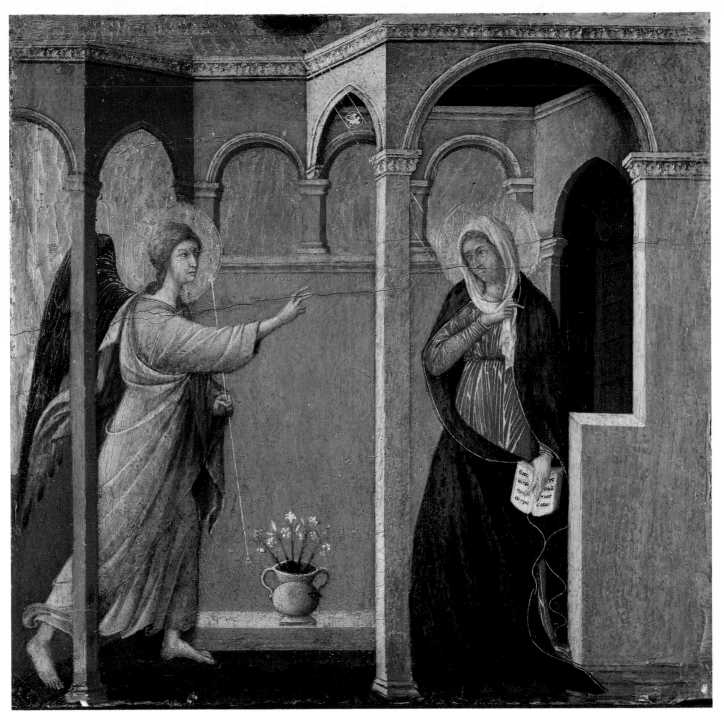

DUCCIO DI BUONINSEGNA
born and died Siena, active 1278 – died 1319
The Annunciation (predella panel from the *Maestà* altarpiece) c 1308/11
wood 43.2 × 43.8
Inscribed in Latin on the book held by the Virgin, from Isaiah vii 14:
 'Behold, a virgin shall conceive, and bear a son and shall call his
 name . . .'
Purchased 1883

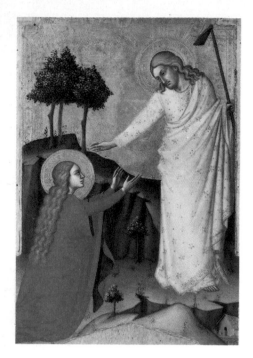

Style of ANDREA DE CIONE called ORCAGNA
active Florence c 1343, died 1368/69
Noli me tangere
wood 55.2 × 37.8
Presented 1924

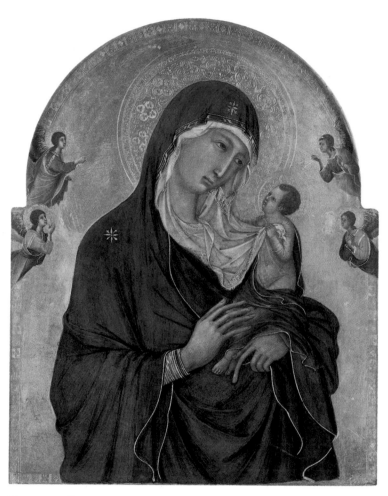

DUCCIO DI BUONINSEGNA
born and died Siena, active 1278 – died 1319
The Virgin and Child (centre panel of a triptych)
   probably before 1308
wood 42.5 × 34.5
Purchased 1857

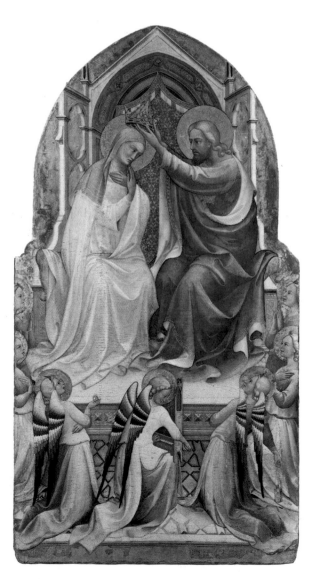

PIERO DI GIOVANNI called DON LORENZO MONACO
born Siena before 1372, died Florence 1422/24
The Coronation of the Virgin (centre portion of an
   altarpiece) c 1415
wood 217.2 × 115.6
Purchased 1902

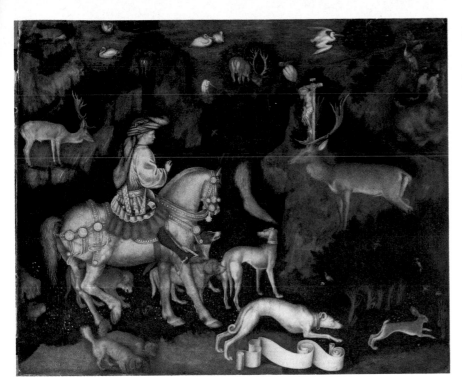

ANTONIO PISANO called PISANELLO
born Verona before 1395, died Naples 1455(?)
The Vision of St Eustace
wood 54.6 × 65.4
Purchased 1895

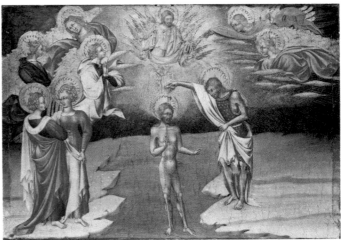

GIOVANNI DI PAOLO
born and died Siena, c1403 –1482
The Baptism of Christ (predella panel
  from an altarpiece)
wood 30.8 × 44.5
Purchased 1944

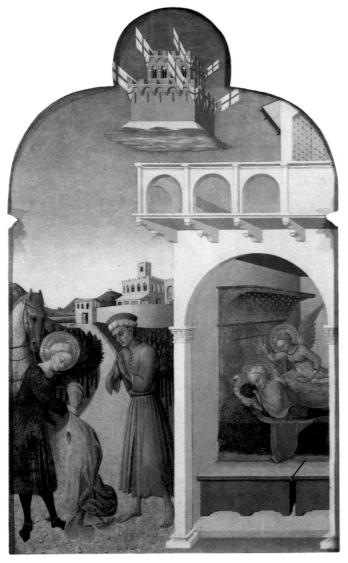

STEFANO DI GIOVANNI called SASSETTA
born and died Siena, 1392(?)–1450
The whim of the young St Francis to become a soldier
(panel from an altarpiece) probably 1437/44
wood 87 × 52.4
Purchased 1934

15

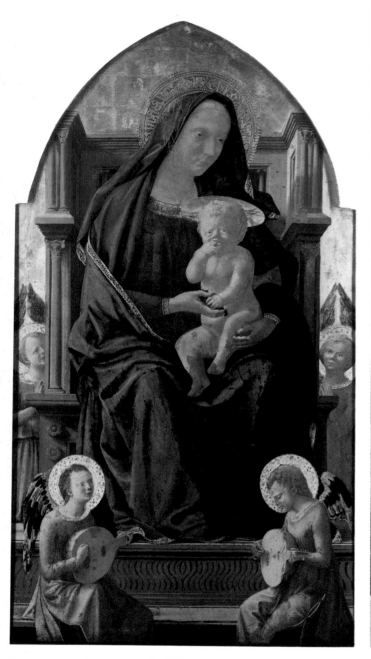
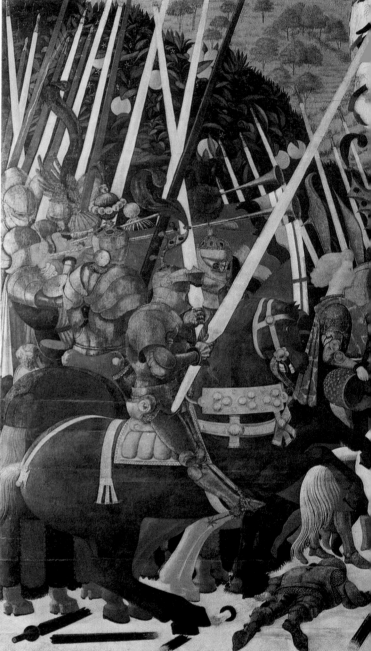

Tommaso di Giovanni called Masaccio
born San Giovanni Valdarno 1401, died Rome 1427/29
The Virgin and Child (centre panel of a polyptych) 1426
wood 135.3 × 73
Purchased 1916

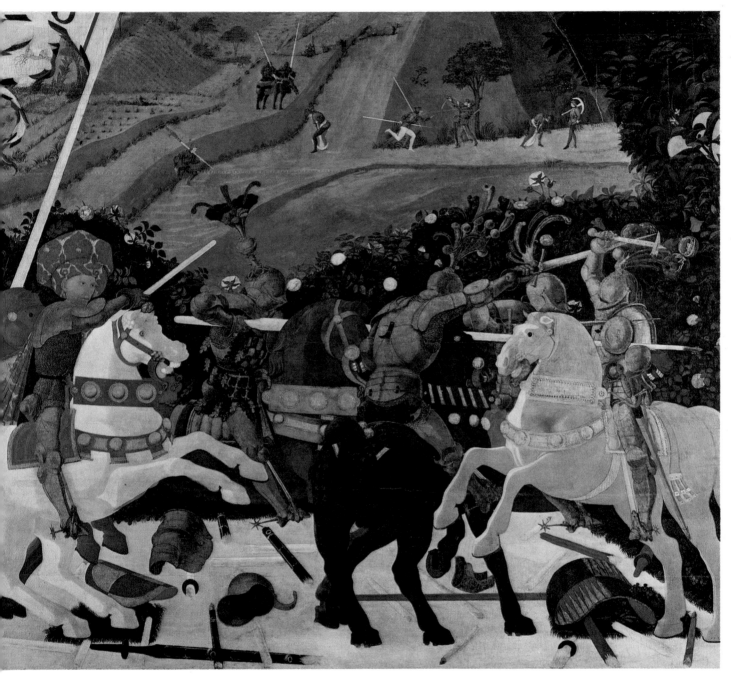

PAOLO DI DONO called UCCELLO
born and died Florence, c 1397–1475
The Battle of San Romano c 1435/50
wood 181.6 × 320
Purchased 1857

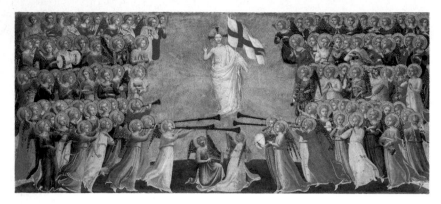

GUIDO DI PIETRO called FRA ANGELICO
born Vicchio 1387, died Rome 1455
Christ Glorified in the Court of Heaven (centre panel of
 the predella from an altarpiece) c 1435
wood 31.8 × 73
Purchased 1860

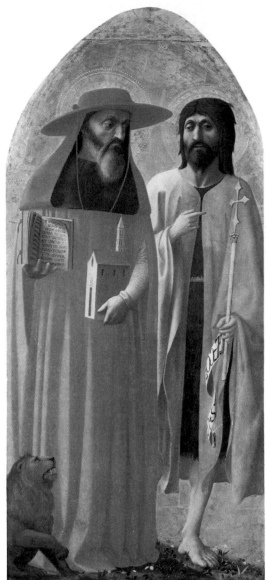

Ascribed to MASOLINO
born Panicale c 1383, died after 1432
St John the Baptist and St Jerome
(wing of a triptych painted on both faces) c 1428/31
wood 114.3 × 54.6
Purchased 1950

FRA FILIPPO LIPPI
born Florence c 1406(?), died Spoleto 1469
The Annunciation c 1448(?)
wood 68.6 × 152.4
Presented 1861

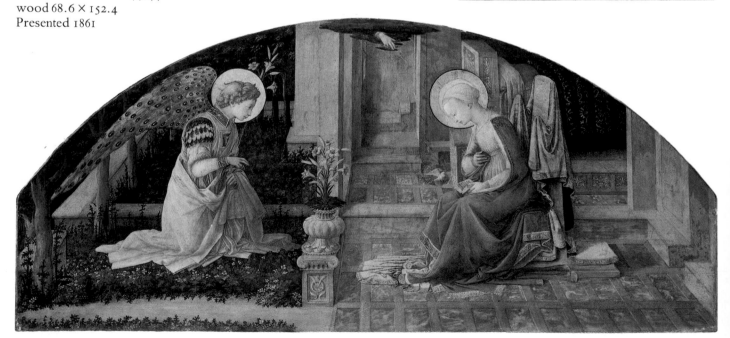

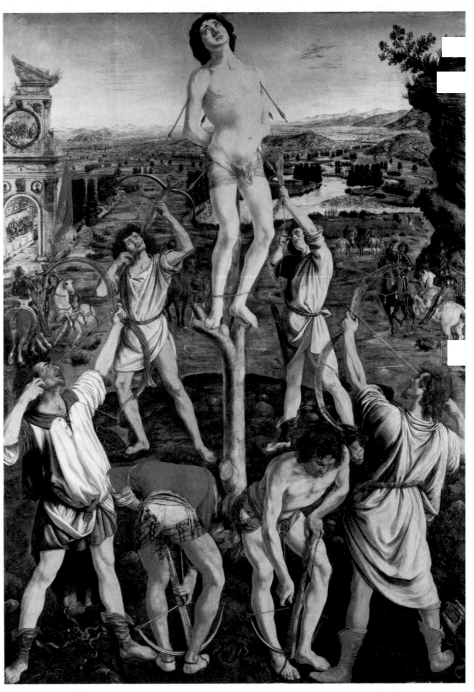

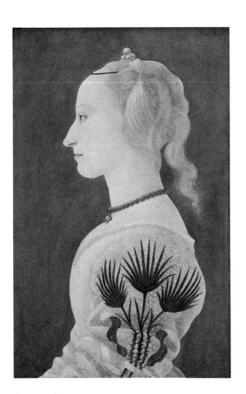

ALESSO BALDOVINETTI
born and died Florence,
c 1426–1499
Portrait of a lady c 1465
wood 62.9 × 40.6
Purchased 1866

Ascribed to the brothers ANTONIO and PIERO DEL POLLAIUOLO
both born and died Florence, c 1432–1498, c 1441–1496
The Martyrdom of St Sebastian (altarpiece) c 1475
wood 291.5 × 202.6
Purchased 1857

PIERO DELLA FRANCESCA
born and died Borgo San Sepolcro,
1410/20–1492
The Nativity a late work
wood 124.4 × 122.6
Purchased 1874

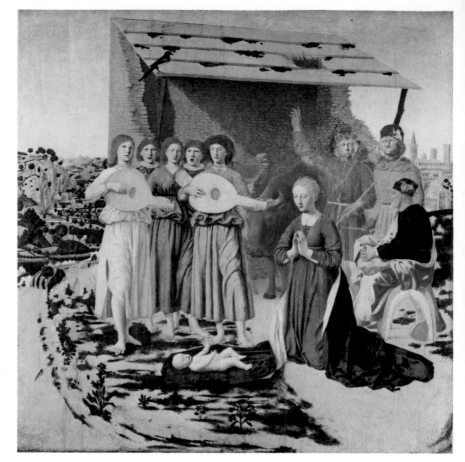

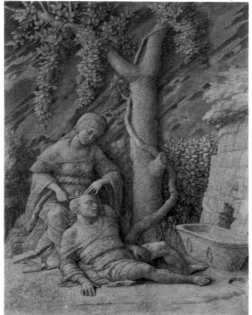

ANDREA MANTEGNA
born Isola di Carturo c 1430/31,
died Mantua 1506
Samson and Delilah a late work
linen 47 × 36.8
Inscribed in Latin with a proverb:
'Woman is evil, a trifle worse than the
devil'
Purchased 1883

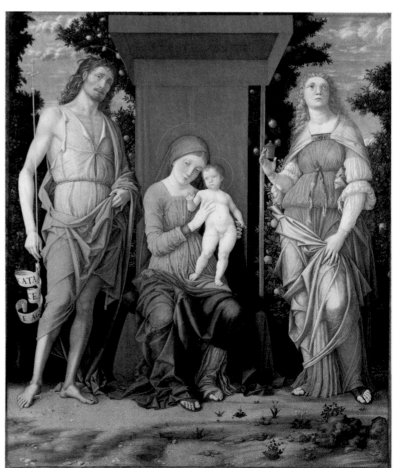

ANDREA MANTEGNA
born Isola di Carturo c 1430/31, died Mantua 1506
*The Virgin and Child with the Magdalen and St John
the Baptist* (altarpiece) c 1469(?)
canvas 139.1 × 116.8
signed
Purchased 1855

CARLO GIOVANNI CRIVELLI
born Venice between 1435/40, died Ascoli Piceno 1493
The Annunciation with St Emidius (altarpiece) 1486
canvas, transferred from wood 207 × 146.7
signed and dated
Presented 1864

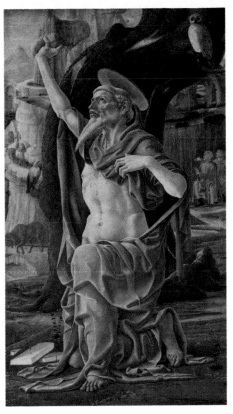

COSIMO TURA
born and died Ferrara, c 1431–1495
St Jerome (fragment)
wood 101 × 57.2
Purchased 1867

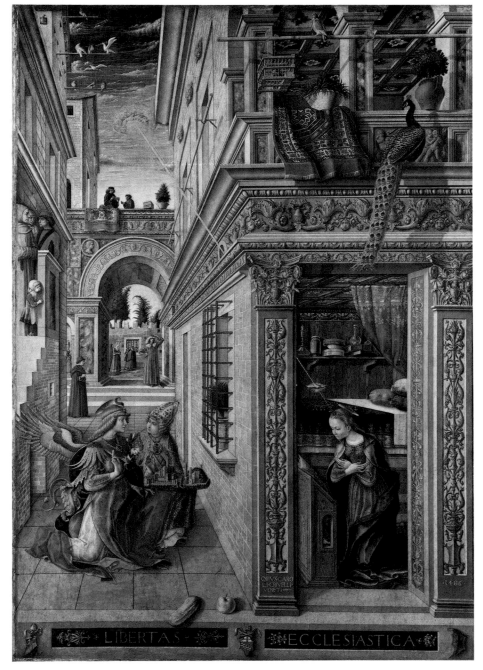

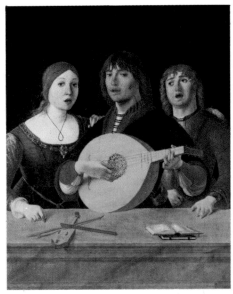

LORENZO COSTA
born Ferrara 1459/60, died Mantua 1535
A concert an early work
wood 95.3 × 75.6
Bequeathed 1910

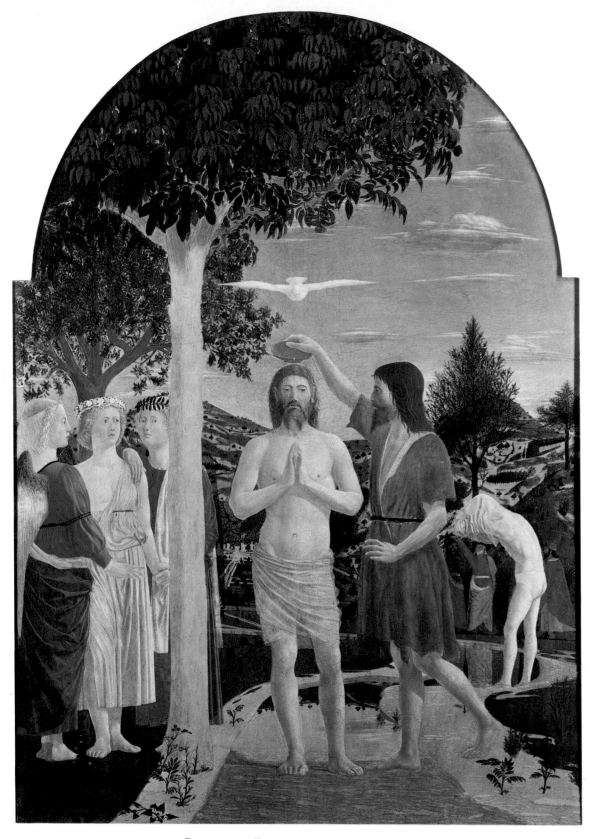

PIERO DELLA FRANCESCA
born and died Borgo San Sepolcro, 1410/20–1492
The Baptism of Christ (part of an altarpiece) an early work
wood 167.6 × 116.2
Purchased 1861

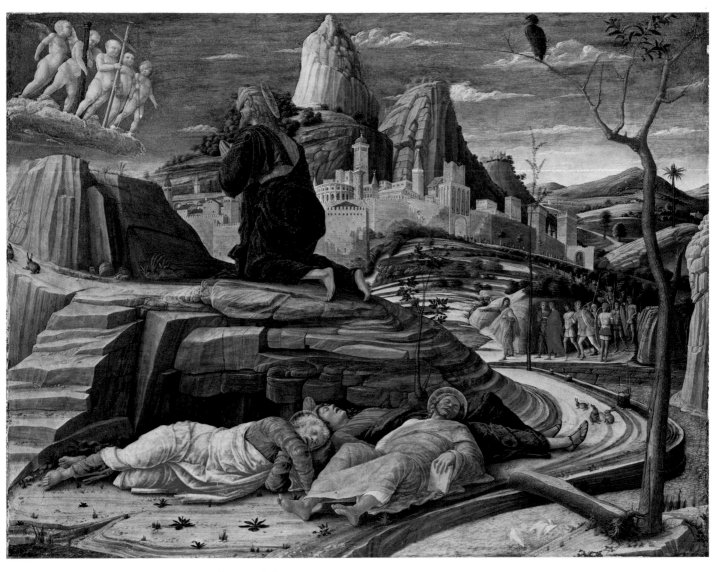

ANDREA MANTEGNA
born Isola di Carturo c 1430/31, died Mantua 1506
The Agony in the Garden 1460s(?)
wood 62.9 × 80
signed
Purchased 1894

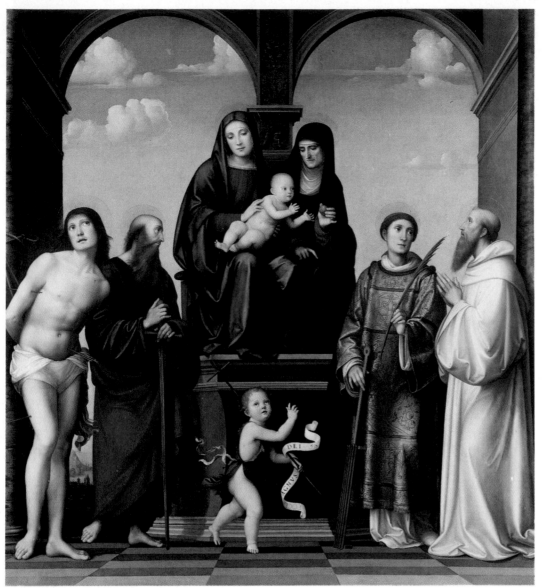

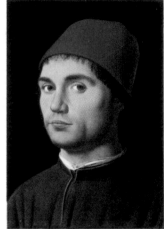

FRANCESCO RAIBOLINI called
    FRANCIA
born and died Bologna,
    c 1450–1517/18
*The Virgin and Child with
    Saints* (altarpiece) c 1511
canvas, transferred from
wood 195 × 180.5
Purchased 1841

ANTONELLO DA MESSINA
born and died Messina,
    c 1430–1479
Portrait of a man c 1475
wood 35.6 × 25.4
Purchased 1883

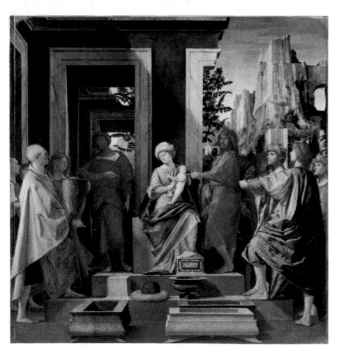

BARTOLOMEO SUARDI
    called BRAMANTINO
born and died Milan,
    1450/55–1530
*The Adoration of the
    Kings* probably
    1490
wood 56.8 × 55
Bequeathed 1916

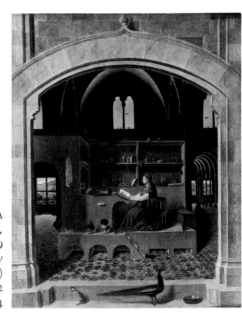

ANTONELLO DA MESSINA
born and died Messina,
    c 1430–1479
St Jerome in his study
    c 1456(?)
wood 45.7 × 36.2
Purchased 1894

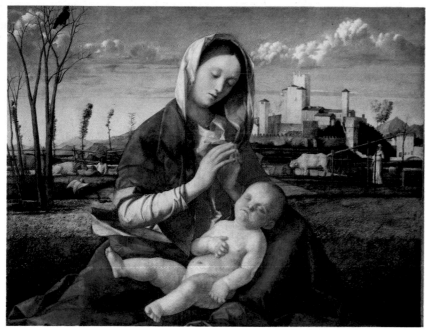

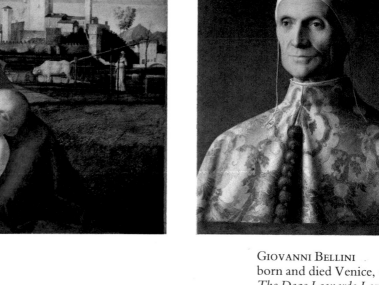

GIOVANNI BELLINI
born and died Venice, c 1430–1516
The Madonna of the Meadow a late work
board, transferred from wood
67.3 × 86.4
Purchased 1858

GIOVANNI BELLINI
born and died Venice, c 1430–1516
The Agony in the Garden c 1465
wood 81.3 × 127
Purchased 1863

GIOVANNI BELLINI
born and died Venice, c 1430–1516
The Doge Leonardo Loredan c 1501
wood 61.6 × 45.1
signed
Purchased 1844

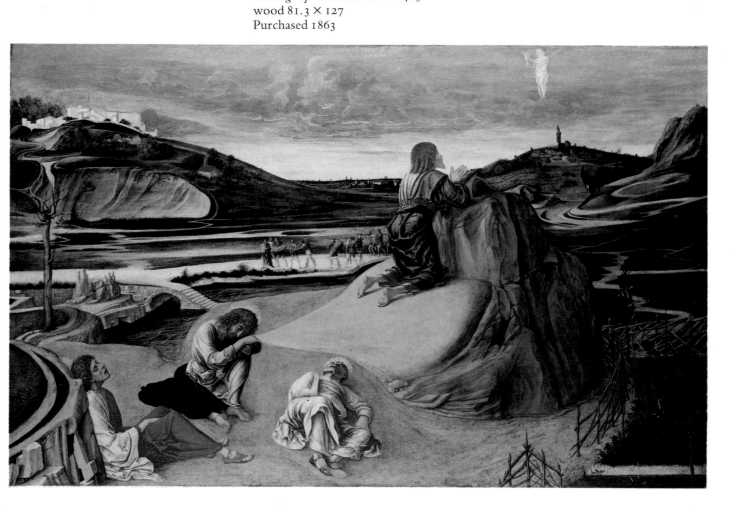

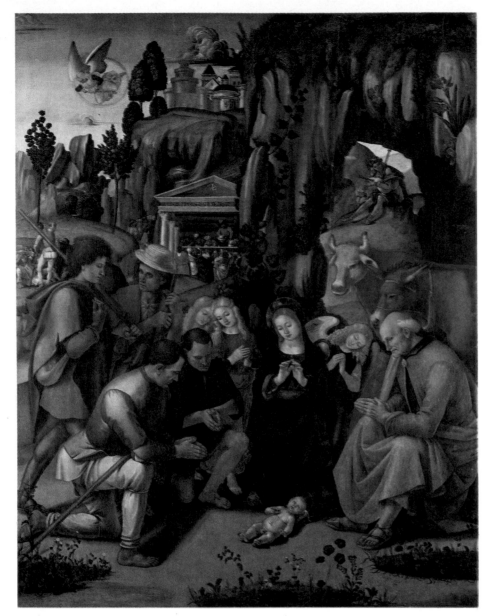

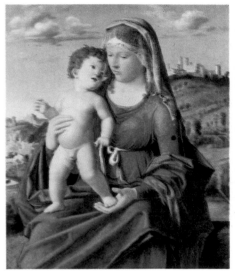

GIOVANNI BATTISTA CIMA DA
 CONEGLIANO
born Conegliano 1459/60, died Venice
 1517/18
The Virgin and Child
wood 69.2 × 57.2
signed
Purchased 1858

LUCA SIGNORELLI
born and died Cortona, 1441(?)–1523
The Adoration of the Shepherds
(altarpiece) probably 1496
wood 215.9 × 170.2
signed
Purchased 1882

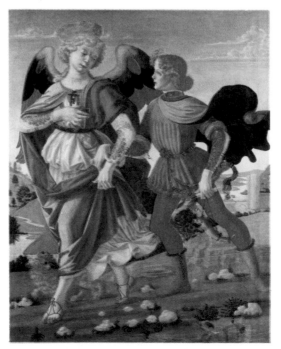

Follower of ANDREA DEL VERROCCHI
born Florence c 1435, died Venice 14
Tobias and the Angel early 1470s(?)
wood 83.9 × 66
Purchased 1867

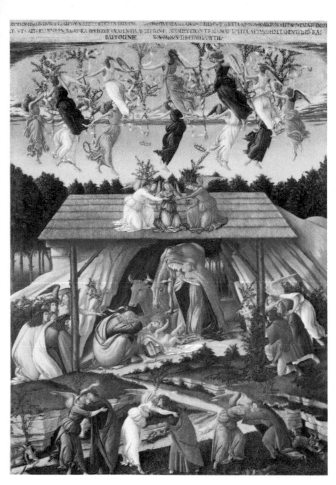

ALESSANDRO DI MARIANO FILIPEPI called SANDRO BOTTICELLI
born and died Florence, c 1445–1510
The Mystic Nativity c 1500
canvas 108.6 × 74.9
Inscription at the top is in Greek, the precise interpretation is
obscure: 'I Sandro painted this picture at the end of the year
1500(?) in the troubles of Italy in the half time according to the
11th Chapter of St John in the second woe of the Apocalypse in
the loosing of the devil for three and a half years then he will be
chained in the 12th Chapter and we shall see clearly (?) . . . as in
this picture'
Purchased 1878

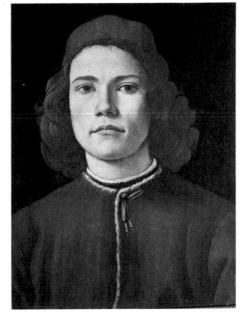

ALESSANDRO DI MARIANO FILIPEPI
called SANDRO BOTTICELLI
born and died Florence,
c 1445–1510
Portrait of a young man c 1482(?)
wood 37.5 × 28.3
Purchased 1859

ALESSANDRO DI MARIANO FILIPEPI
called SANDRO BOTTICELLI
born and died Florence, c 1445–1510
Venus and Mars 1480s(?)
wood 69.2 × 173.4
Purchased 1874

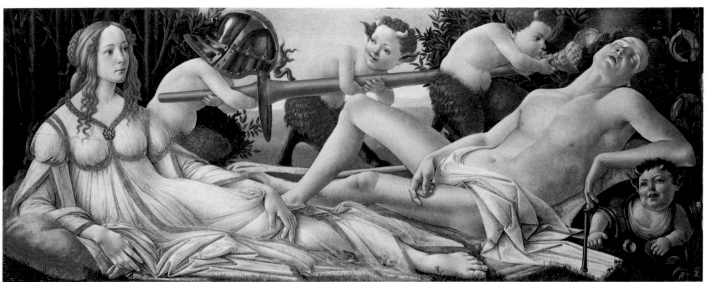

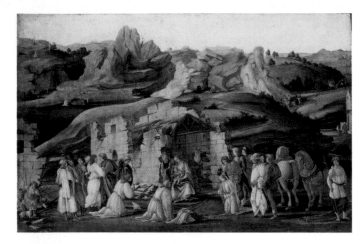

FILIPPINO LIPPI
born Prato 1457(?), died Florence 1504
The Adortion of the Kings an early work
wood 57.5 × 85.7
Purchased 1882

PIERO DI COSIMO
born and died Florence, c 1462–1521
A mythological subject
wood 65.4 × 184.2
Purchased 1862

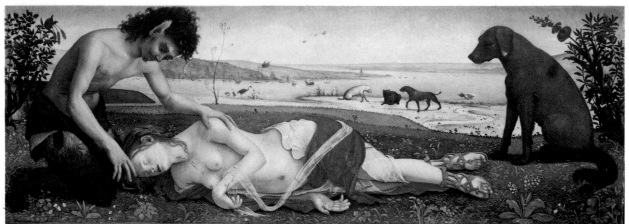

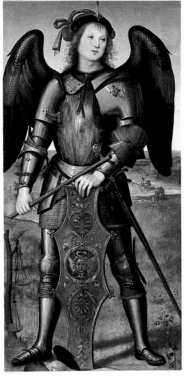
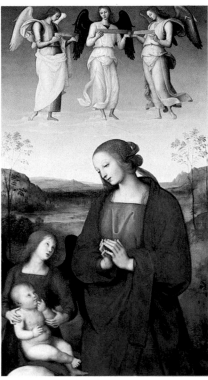
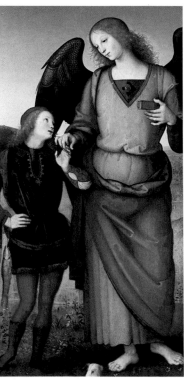

PIETRO VANNUCCI called PERUGINO
born Città della Pieve c 1445/50, died Fontignano 1523
The Virgin and Child with St Raphael and St Michael (three panels of an altarpiece) begun c 1496
left panel 114 × 56, centre panel 113 × 64, right panel 113 × 56 signed
Purchased 1856

Early northern schools

The collection of early Netherlandish and German pictures at the National Gallery is very much smaller than the early Italian collection, yet it contains a large proportion of works of the highest quality, by Jan van Eyck, Rogier van der Weyden, Memlinc and Holbein to mention only the most familiar names. There are nevertheless notable absences; sixteenth-century Flanders is only represented by a few artists, for example Jan Gossaert (p 38), and the Gallery possesses hardly any post-Renaissance German works.

Fortunately, however, the revival of interest in 'primitive' painters in the middle of the nineteenth century extended beyond the Italian schools to the early masters of the north, and from the 1840s a slow stream of Netherlandish and German pictures began to trickle into the National Gallery. Yet they never received the earnest attention devoted to the Italian fifteenth century, and most of the pictures illustrated in this section were acquired this century. It is only comparatively recently that the concept of the Renaissance has been expanded to include the revolution in painting that occurred in Flanders in the fifteenth century and a little later in Germany, and perhaps only now are the works of van Eyck and van der Weyden granted a status equal to that of their southern contemporaries. It is recognised today that the artists of the north did more than imitate the discoveries made in Italy, and that in the development of realism and the formulation of oil-painting they in fact anticipated the achievements of the Italian fifteenth century. Antonello da Messina and Giovanni Bellini, two seminal figures in the Italian Renaissance, both owed much to the Netherlandish painting they knew from examples brought to Italy.

The Renaissance in the north was less indebted to the classic art of Greece and Rome. In Bruges, and later in Brussels and Antwerp, economic expansion increased the demand for works of art and led to rapid developments in painting. There was a move away from the flat, linear conventions of Gothic art to a detailed modern realism, in which distinct human types are of central importance. Jan van Eyck built on the advances made by Robert Campin (p 32), and his *Arnolfini Marriage* (p 34), one of the first early Netherlandish paintings to enter the Collection, illustrates his achievement in formulating a system which is naturalistic in its details and in its placing of figures and objects within a defined space. It is signed by the artist, who, unlike the anonymous medieval craftsman of the previous century, now dares, as it were, to proclaim his presence in his work. His *Man in a turban* (p 33) may be a self-portrait, and in it we can observe the new realism at its most accomplished. The folds of the turban are minutely observed, and in the finely painted features we find, virtually for the first time, the portrayal of a specific personality, neither schematized nor idealized.

The first German picture to enter the Collection was the portrait by Baldung (p 41) then attributed to Dürer. Purchased at Eastlake's insistence in 1854, just before the reconstitution of the Gallery, it is indicative of the new emphasis then being given to the purchase of earlier works. In the same year the Krüger collection, which consisted chiefly of early German pictures, was bought at Minden, and these works still represent a considerable part of the German collection at the National Gallery. Among them were six fragments of an altarpiece by the Master of Liesborn, including *The Annunciation* (p 40), and other works from his circle. The altarpiece had been installed in the Abbey Church at Liesborn in Westphalia by 1490 and remained there until the early nineteenth century. Less naturalistic in style than such contemporary Netherlandish painting as the triptych by Memlinc (p 35), it shows the influence of the important fifteenth-century Cologne School, particularly in the elegant poses of the figures and the decorative treatment of architecture and costume.

More German pictures, including examples from Cologne, were presented to the Gallery in 1863 by Queen Victoria at the wish of the Prince Consort. Prince Albert, a friend of Eastlake, was largely responsible for the growth of interest in 'primitive' painting, both Italian and Northern. Among his pictures which entered the Gallery in that year were the wing of an altarpiece by the Master of the St Bartholomew Altarpiece showing St Peter and

St Dorothy (p 40), a fine late work of the Cologne School, and a panel by the most famous master of Cologne, Stephan Lochner, which shows the Gothic style still flourishing in Germany at the middle of the fifteenth century.

A painting which shows German art at a more developed stage is the portrait attributed to Dürer, depicting his father (p 42). This penetrating study of character (the authorship of which is still questioned) was presented to Charles I by the city of Nuremberg in 1636 and was purchased by the Gallery in 1904. The first Holbein to enter the Collection was the famous 'Ambassadors' (p 44) purchased in 1890. This painting had been in English possession since its execution, as had the portrait of *Christina of Denmark* (p 44) which was saved from leaving the nation in 1909 when the National Art-Collections Fund succeeded in purchasing it for the Gallery. The portrait shows the young widow of the Duke of Milan, whom Henry VIII in 1538 was hoping to take as his fourth wife. From a study Holbein made that year in Brussels he produced this full-length portrait for the King, but in 1540 Henry married Anne of Cleves and the Duchess probably never saw Holbein's painting of her.

Another German masterpiece of the Renaissance was acquired by the Gallery as recently as 1980. *Christ taking leave of His Mother* (p 43) by Albrecht Altdorfer, which had been in the Wernher collection at Luton Hoo, was purchased with the aid of grants from the National Heritage Memorial Fund, the Pilgrim Trust and the National Art-Collections Fund. It is one of only two works by this rare and original painter in the country (the other being a small landscape also in the National Gallery) and combines a richly varied figure group and a fully elaborated landscape setting of mountains, forest and ruins with a mood of heightened drama and emotion. Altdorfer is especially skilful in his realistic interpretation of natural effects, abundant in this large panel.

The National Art-Collections Fund has on many occasions since its foundation in 1903 helped to acquire works of exceptional quality and importance which would otherwise have almost certainly left the country. In 1929 it contributed to the purchase of one of the most valued objects in the Collection, 'The Wilton Diptych' (p 31). This work, which had been in the collection of the Earls of Pembroke at Wilton House since the eighteenth century, shows Richard II, King of England from 1377 to 1399, being presented to the Virgin and Child by his patron saints. It is generally thought to be French in origin and may have been painted for the King to commemorate his marriage to Isabella of France in 1396. In its elaborate and decorative description of detail and its rich gem-like colouring, 'The Wilton Diptych' is representative of the International Gothic style that flourished throughout Europe in the early fifteenth century. Features of this style are seen not only in paintings of the northern artists, but also in the work of early Italian masters such as Pisanello and Uccello.

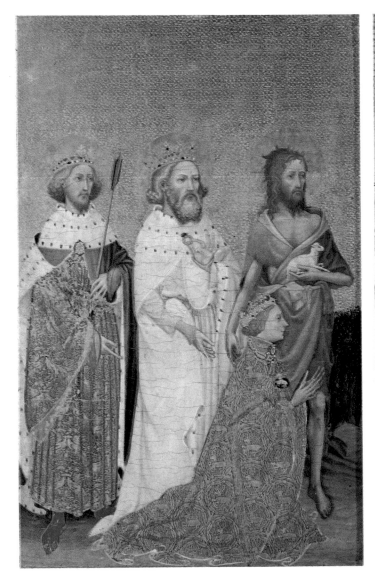 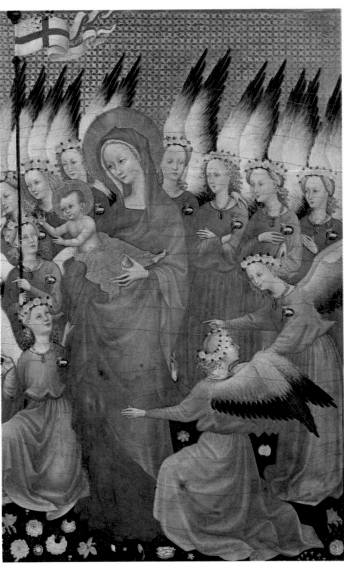

FRENCH SCHOOL
Richard II presented to the Virgin and Child by his patron saints
  'The Wilton Diptych' c 1395 or later
wood each panel 45.7 × 29.2
Purchased 1929

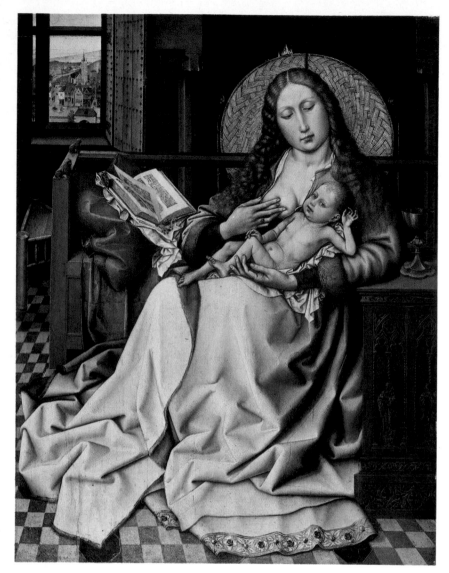

ROBERT CAMPIN
born and died Tournai, 1378/79–1444
The Virgin and Child before a firescreen
before 1430
wood 63.5 × 49.5
Bequeathed 1910

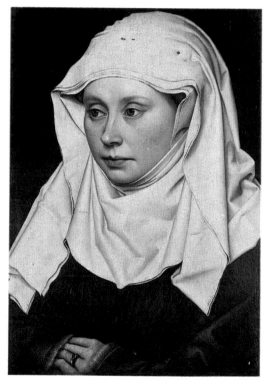

Ascribed to ROBERT CAMPIN
born and died Tournai, 1378/79–1444
A woman an early work
wood 40.7 × 27.9
Purchased 1860

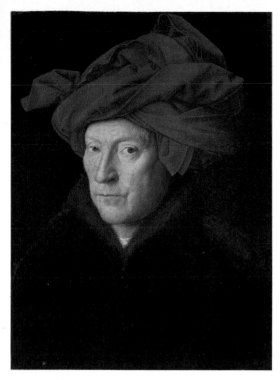

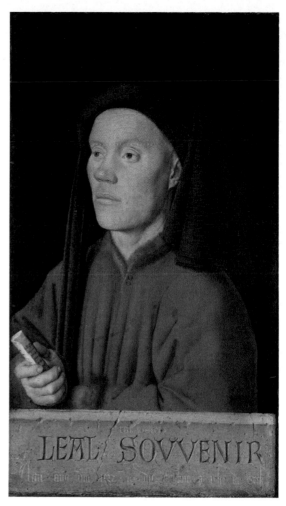

JAN VAN EYCK
born Maaseyck c 1390, died Bruges 1441
A Man in a Turban 1433
wood 33.3 × 25.8
signed and dated
Purchased 1851

JAN VAN EYCK
born Maaseyck c 1390, died Bruges 1441
Portrait of a young man 1432
wood 34.4 × 19
signed and dated
Purchased 1857

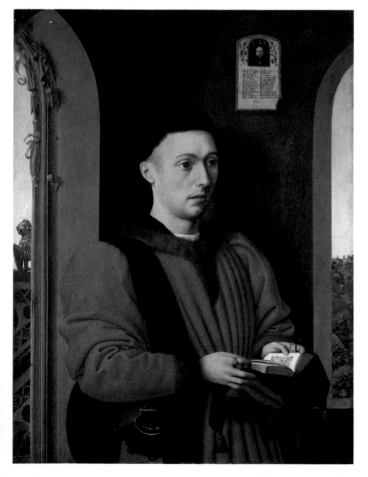

PETRUS CHRISTUS
born Baerle, active 1442, died Bruges 1472/3
Portrait of a young man c 1450/60
wood 35.6 × 26.4
Bequeathed 1910

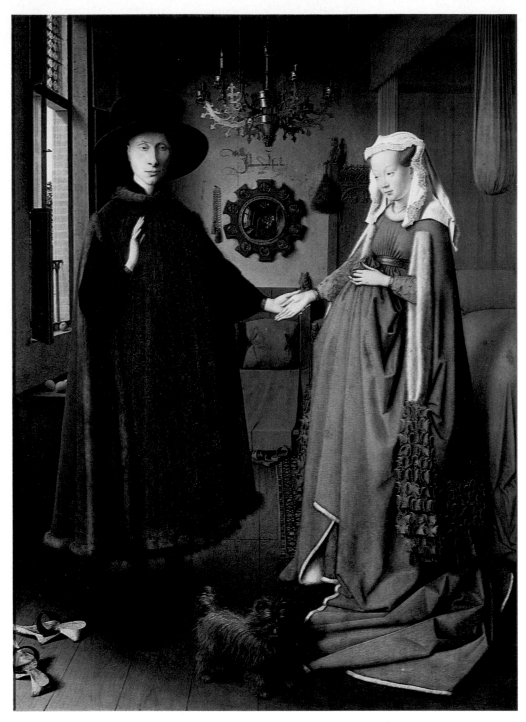

JAN VAN EYCK
born Maaseyck c 1390, died Bruges 1441
The Arnolfini Marriage 1434
wood 81.8 × 59.7
signed and dated
Purchased 1842

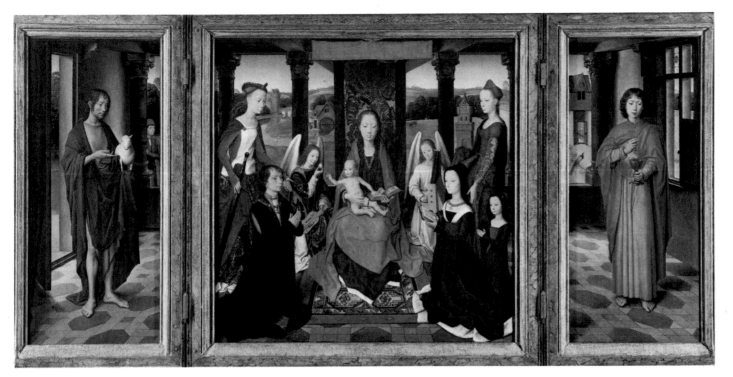

Hans Memlinc
born Mainz 1425/40, died Bruges 1494
The Virgin and Child with saints and donors (triptych) c 1477
wood centre 70.8 × 70.5, wings 71.1 × 30.5
Purchased 1957

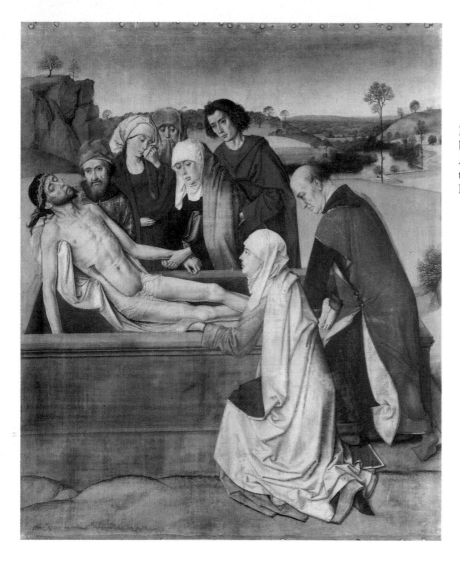

DIERIC BOUTS
born Haarlem c 1415, died Louvain 1475
Entombment an early work
tempera on flax 90.2 × 74.3
Purchased 1860

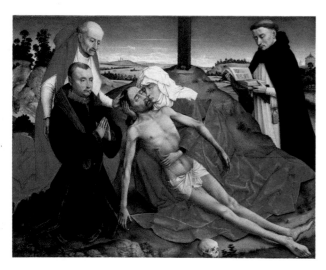

ROGIER VAN DER WEYDEN
born Tournai c 1399, died Brussels 1464
Pietà
wood 35.6 × 45.1
Purchased 1956

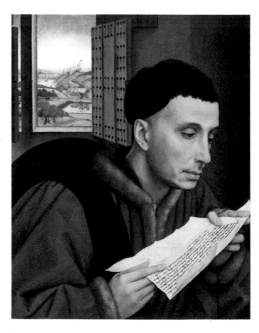

ROGIER VAN DER WEYDEN
born Tournai c 1399, died Brussels 1464
St Ivo c 1450
wood 45.1 × 34.8
Purchased 1971

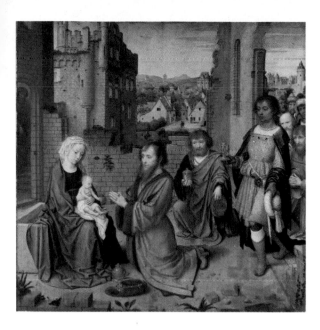

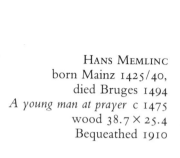

GERARD DAVID
born Oudewater c 1460,
    died Bruges 1523
The Adoration of the Kings
    (panel from an
    altarpiece) after 1515
wood 59.7 × 58.4
Bequeathed 1880

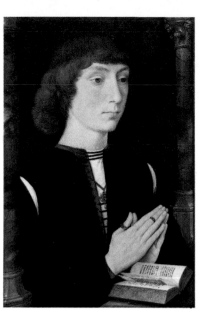

HANS MEMLINC
born Mainz 1425/40,
died Bruges 1494
A young man at prayer c 1475
wood 38.7 × 25.4
Bequeathed 1910

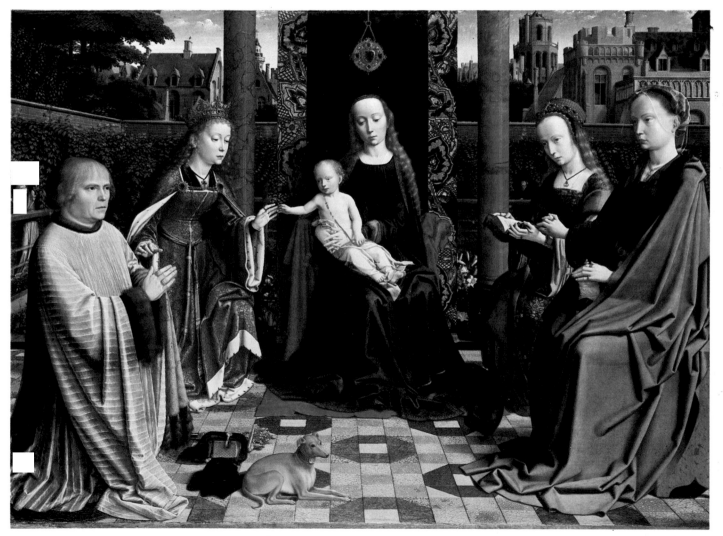

GERARD DAVID
born Oudewater c 1460, died Bruges 1523
Virgin and Child with saints and donor (panel from an altarpiece) c 1505/09
wood 106 × 144.1
Bequeathed 1895

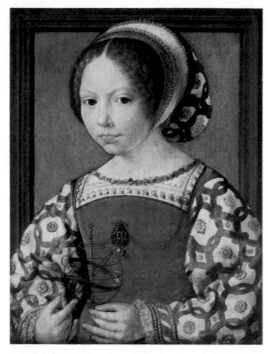

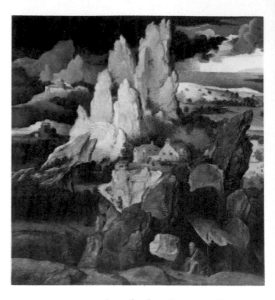

Jan Gossaert called Mabuse
born Maubeuge c 1478, died
    Middleburg 1532
A little girl c 1520(?)
wood 38.1 × 28.9
Purchased 1908

Ascribed to Joachim Patenier
born Bouvignes c 1485, died
    Antwerp not later than 1524
St Jerome in a rocky landscape
wood 36.2 × 34.3
Bequeathed 1936

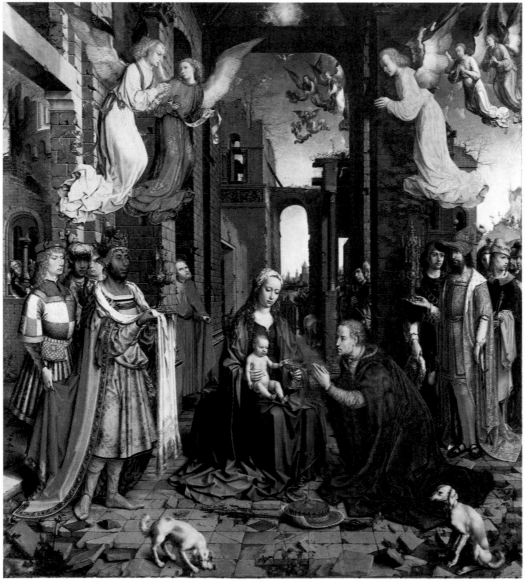

Jan Gossaert called Mabuse
born Maubeuge c 1478, died
    Middleburg 1532
The Adoration of the Kings
    c 1506
wood 177.2 × 161.3
signed
Purchased 1911

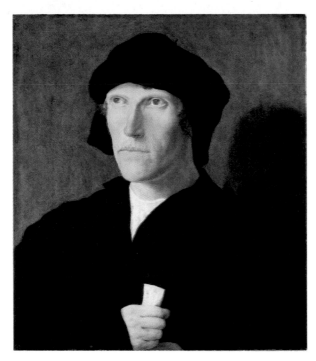

LUCAS VAN LEYDEN
born and died Leyden, c 1494–1533
A man aged thirty-eight c 1521
wood 47.6 × 40.6
Inscribed on the paper in the sitter's hand: 38
Presented 1921

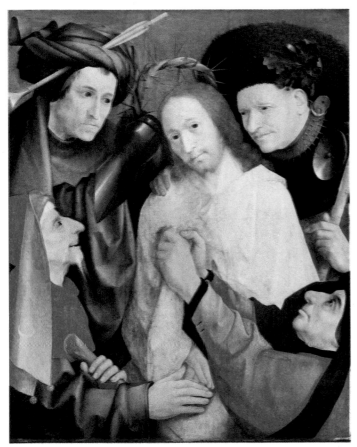

HIERONYMUS BOSCH
born and died Bois-le-Duc, 1450/60–1516
Christ mocked probably an early work
wood 73.5 × 59.1
Purchased 1934

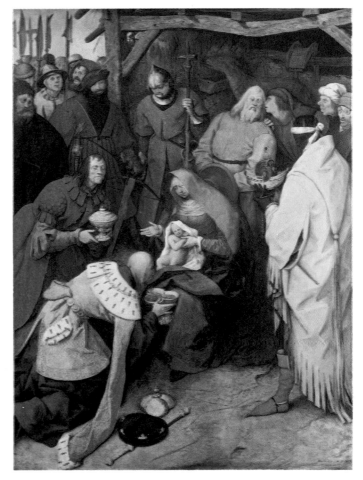

PIETER BRUEGEL THE ELDER
born Campin c 1525, died Brussels 1569
The Adoration of the Kings 1564
wood 111.1 × 83.2
signed and dated
Purchased 1920

MASTER OF THE ST BARTHOLOMEW ALTARPIECE
born and died Cologne, active late 15th/early 16th century
St Peter and St Dorothy (panel from an altarpiece) a late work
wood 125.7 × 71.1
Presented 1863

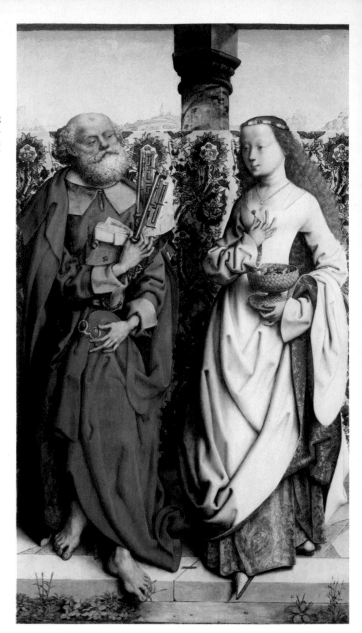

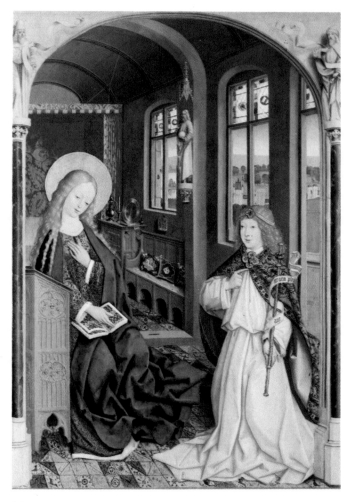

MASTER OF LIESBORN
Westphalia, active second half of the 15th century
The Annunciation (panel from an altarpiece) c 1480
wood 98.7 × 70.5
Purchased 1854

STEPHAN LOCHNER
born Meersburg 1405/15, died Cologne 1451
St Matthew, St Catherine and St John the Evangelist
(wing of an altarpiece) a late work
wood 68.6 × 58.1
Presented 1863

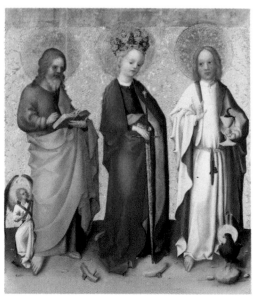

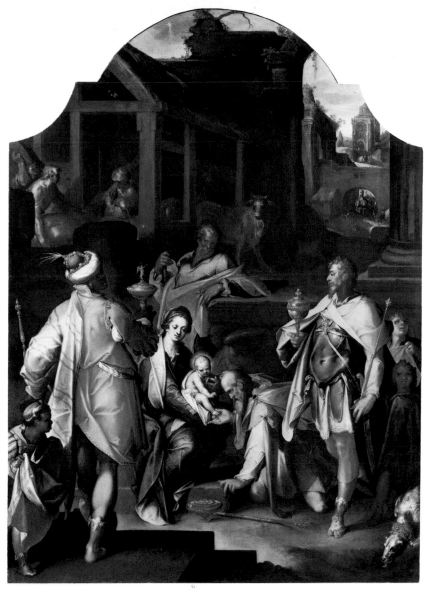

BARTHOLOMEUS SPRANGER
born Antwerp 1546, died Prague 1611
The Adoration of the Kings c 1595
canvas 199.8 × 143.7
signed
Purchased 1970

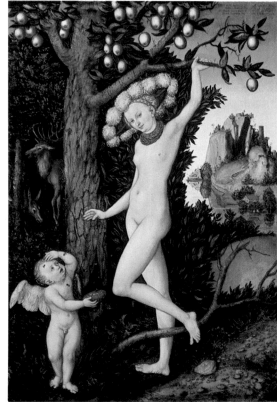

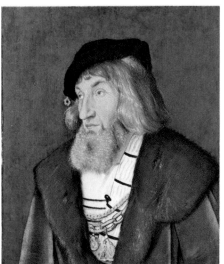

HANS BALDUNG GRIEN
born Gmünd 1484/85, died
  Strasbourg 1545
Portrait of a man 1514
wood 59.3 × 48.9
dated
Purchased 1854

LUCAS CRANACH THE ELDER
born Kronach 1472, died
Weimer 1553
Cupid complaining to Venus after
1522(?)
wood 81.3 × 54.6
signed
Purchased 1963

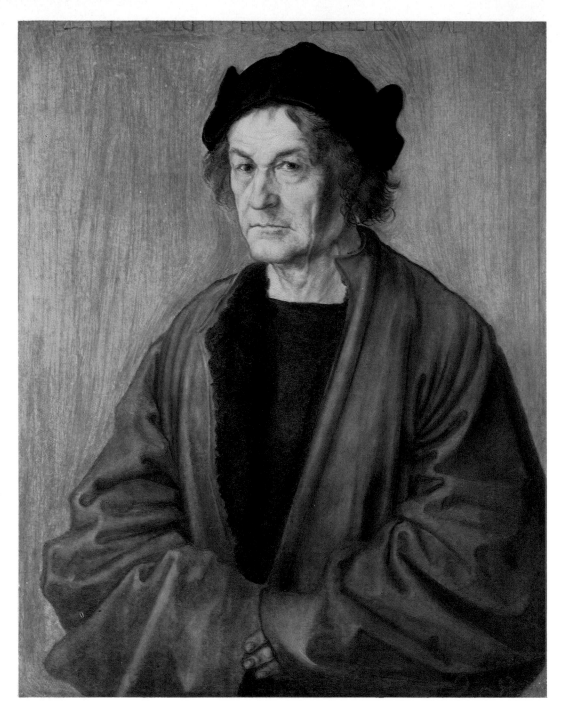

Ascribed to ALBRECHT DÜRER
born and died Nuremburg, 1471–1528
The painter's father 1497
wood 51 × 40.3
dated
Purchased 1904

ALBRECHT ALTDORFER
born and died Regensburg, c 1480–1538
Christ taking leave of His Mother a mature work
wood 140 × 110
Purchased 1980

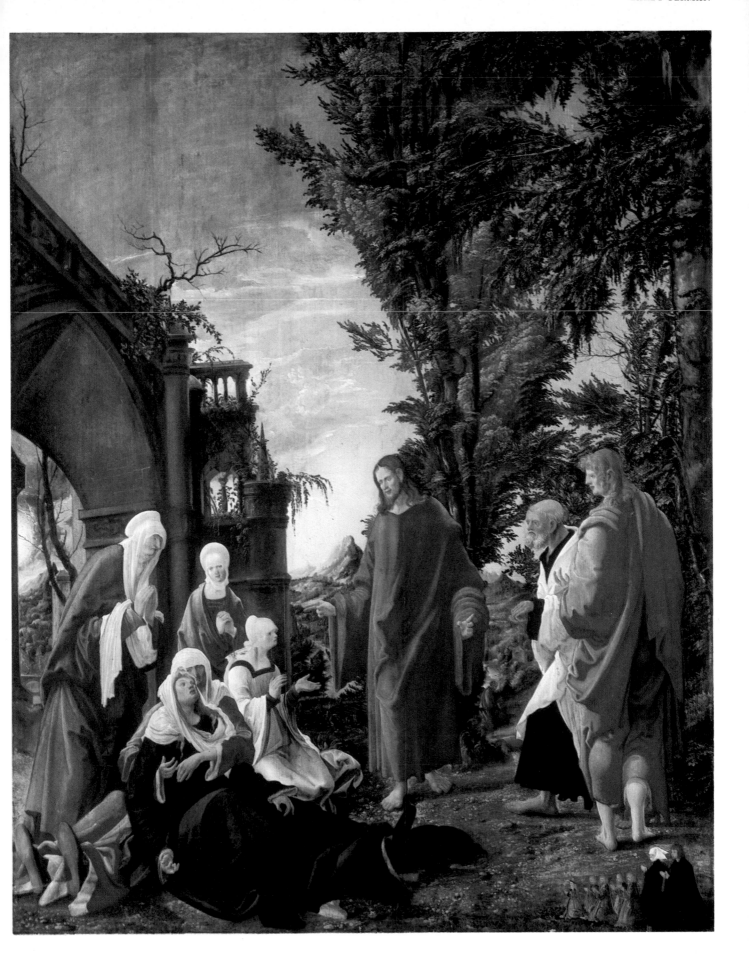

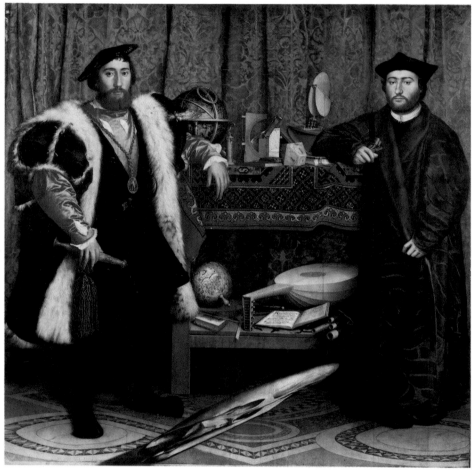

HANS HOLBEIN THE YOUNGER
born Augsburg 1497/98, died London 1543
Jean de Dinteville and Georges de Selve, 'The Ambassadors' 1533
wood 207 × 209.5
signed and dated
Purchased 1890

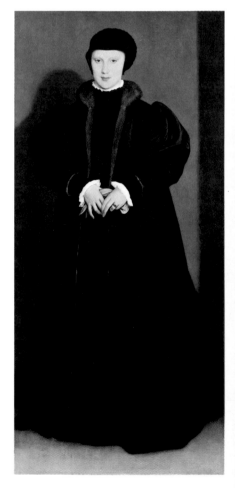

HANS HOLBEIN THE YOUNGER
born Augsburg 1497/98, died London 1543
Christina of Denmark, Duchess of Milan
probably 1538
wood 179.1 × 82.6
Presented 1909

Sixteenth-century Italy

The National Gallery is rare and fortunate in that it possesses fine examples of virtually all the major Italian artists of the High Renaissance. In its very first years the Gallery acquired by purchase, gift and bequest a group of sixteenth-century Italian pictures which remains one of its chief glories. Catalogued number one in the Gallery's inventory is the enormous altarpiece of *The Raising of Lazarus* (p 53) by Sebastiano del Piombo, one of the Angerstein pictures bought in 1824. Michelangelo provided his protégé Sebastiano with studies for parts of this picture, which was executed in 1517/19 in competition with Raphael's *Transfiguration* now in the Vatican Museum. In 1825 the Treasury purchased the Gallery's first Correggio, *The Madonna of the basket* (p 50), and in 1834 two more were added, an *Ecce Homo* and 'The School of Love' (p 50). It seems that this latter picture was intended to represent spiritual love, in contrast to its pendant, the *Antiope* in the Louvre, which shows carnal love.

Titian's *Bacchus and Ariadne* (p 56), one of the three Bacchanals which he painted for Alfonso d'Este, Duke of Ferrara, was purchased in 1826, and demonstrates not only his mastery of movement, but also his dramatic use of vibrant colour. In the same year the British Institution presented a Veronese and Parmigianino's large altarpiece of *The Madonna and Child with St John the Baptist and St Jerome* (p 54), painted when the artist was only twenty years old. Among the pictures bequeathed by the Reverend Holwell Carr in 1831 were the *St George and the Dragon* by Tintoretto (p 60), a comparatively small work by the artist which shows his sophisticated use of design and light, Barocci's '*La Madonna del Gatto*' (p 59) and an early Titian, *The Holy Family*.

The keenness with which the Treasury and the Trustees seized at every opportunity to acquire such works and their frequency among the early bequests and gifts to the Gallery indicate how highly they were valued in the early nineteenth century. They had long been collected by the English, and until late in the century the opinion that during the High Renaissance painting had reached its point of perfection was never really questioned. Even when the seventeenth century fell from favour and earlier pictures became popular, the Gallery continued to spend large sums on important sixteenth-century Italian works. In 1857 Eastlake finalised the purchase of Veronese's great *Family of Darius before Alexander* (p 60), which was bought from the Pisani family at Venice for the then colossal sum of £13,650. Veronese lends dignity to his subject and emphasises Alexander's magnanimity towards the conquered Persians by arranging the many and varied figures into a harmoniously balanced composition.

Eastlake's successor, Boxall, succeeded in purchasing in 1868 one of Michelangelo's very rare easel-paintings, *The Entombment* (p 52). According to one account, it had been discovered by its previous owner, the painter Robert Macpherson, as part of a street barrow in Rome. The first Leonardo to enter the Collection was *The Virgin of the Rocks* (p 48), purchased in 1880, an earlier variant of which is in the Louvre, and in 1884 a large altarpiece by Raphael, *The Ansidei Madonna* (p 49), was bought from the Duke of Marlborough for £70,000. Thus before the end of the century the Gallery became one of the few collections to possess important works by Leonardo, Raphael, Michelangelo and Titian, traditionally considered the greatest artists of the period, if not of the whole of western painting.

Recent acquisitions of paintings by these artists illustrate not only the comparative difficulty of obtaining such works nowadays, but also the extraordinary achievement of sixteenth-century Italy. In 1962 Leonardo's famous cartoon of the *Virgin and Child with St Anne and St John the Baptist* (p 47) which had belonged to the Royal Academy since the end of the eighteenth century, was purchased by the National Art-Collections Fund and presented to the Gallery. Dating from around 1500 it marks the attainment of a new aesthetic. The naturalistic detail of fifteenth-century painting here gives way to a more sophisticated and lyrical interpretation of form, where contours are blurred by diffused light to produce an effect which is both mysterious and moving.

A late Titian, *The death of Actaeon* (p 57), as revolutionary in its handling of paint as is the Leonardo cartoon in its drawing, was purchased in 1972. A campaign was mounted to raise the enormous sum required to keep it in the country, and the price of £1.76 million was finally met by a combination of Gallery funds, a special government grant and a large public subscription. In this painting the crisp form and bright colour of the earlier *Bacchus and Ariadne* give way to turbulent, moody paintwork and sombre tones. Diana, gigantic and inhuman in her role as avenger dominates the composition, while against a background of storm-wracked trees the hounds overwhelm the helpless Actaeon, already half-transformed into a stag. At this point, when every means, including the texture of the paint, is used to heighten the expression, painting seems to reach its maturity.

The wonderful richness of colour of Titian's work and that of his contemporaries has been revealed to dramatic effect by the restoration work of the Gallery's Conservation Department over the last thirty years. The *Bacchus and Ariadne* was previously obscured by darkened varnish and retouchings, and Sebastiano's altarpiece of *The Raising of Lazarus* took sixteen years to restore. Originally painted on panel and later transferred to canvas, the altarpiece has eventually been painstakingly secured to a board of stable construction, because the old lining canvas was endangering the painting. Removal of layers of dirt and brown varnish then made visible once again the sombre harmonies of the artists colours. Bronzino's *Allegory* (p 51) gained by the removal of nineteenth-century 'improvements' – fig leaves and draperies added to the nude figures for modesty's sake.

In 1970 one of the original Angerstein pictures was cleaned, revealing a hitherto unrecognised masterpiece. The *Pope Julius II* (p 47) had long been thought only to be one of many early copies of Raphael's portrait, but on cleaning the stunning quality of the revealed paintwork, together with X-ray and other technical information, proved this to be not a copy but Raphael's original. It is another sixteenth-century work of seminal importance for European painting, providing a portrait format that was adopted subsequently by many major artists, including Titian and Velazquez, and a more penetrating study of character than had yet been achieved in paint.

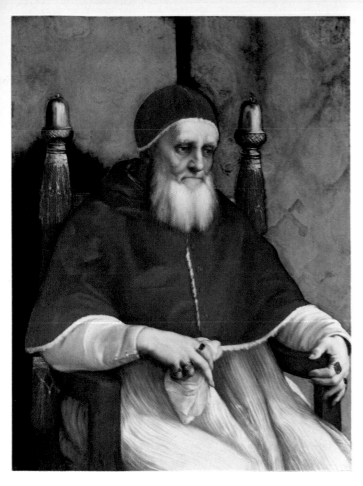

RAFFAELLO SANTI called RAPHAEL
born Urbino 1483, died Rome 1520
Pope Julius II c 1511/12
wood 108 × 80.7
Purchased 1824

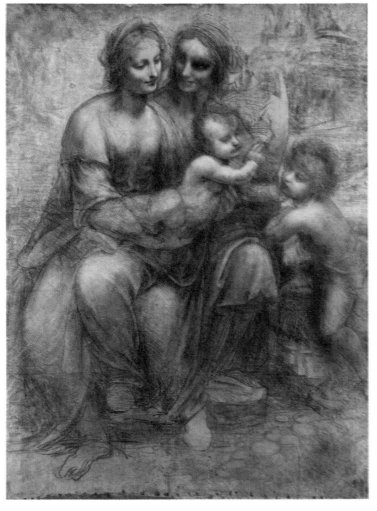

RAFFAELLO SANTI called RAPHAEL
born Urbino 1483, died Rome 1520
St Catherine of Alexandria c 1507
wood 71.5 × 55.7
Purchased 1839

LEONARDO DA VINCI
born Vinci 1452, died Cloux 1519
*Virgin and Child with St Anne and
St John the Baptist* (cartoon) c 1500
black chalk heightened with white on
    paper 141.5 × 104.6
Presented 1962

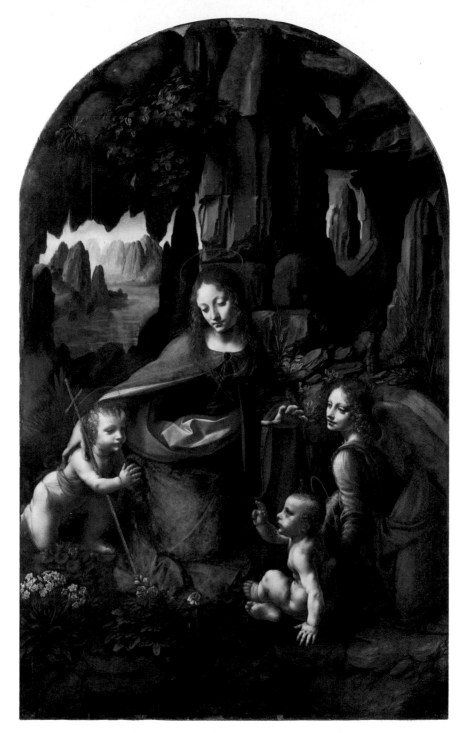

LEONARDO DA VINCI
born Vinci 1452, died Cloux 1519
The Virgin of the Rocks (altarpiece) completed c 1506
wood 189.5 × 120
Purchased 1880

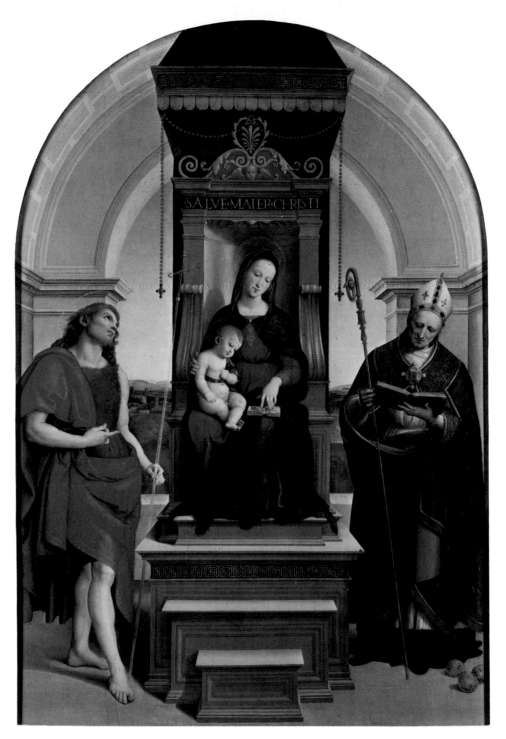

RAFFAELLO SANTI called RAPHAEL
born Urbino 1483, died Rome 1520
The Ansidei Madonna (altarpiece) 1505
wood 209.6 × 148.6
dated
Purchased 1885

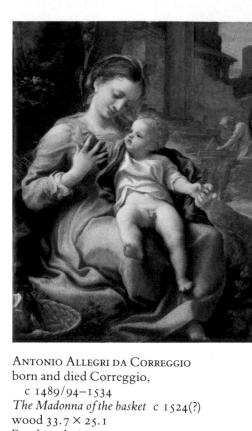

ANTONIO ALLEGRI DA CORREGGIO
born and died Correggio,
  c 1489/94–1534
The Madonna of the basket c 1524(?)
wood 33.7 × 25.1
Purchased 1825

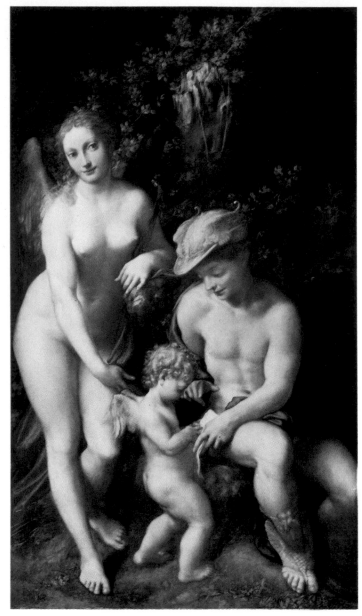

ANTONIO ALLEGRI DA CORREGGIO
born and died Correggio, c 1489/94–1534
*Mercury instructing Cupid before Venus, 'The
  School of Love'* an early work
canvas 155.6 × 91.4
Purchased 1834

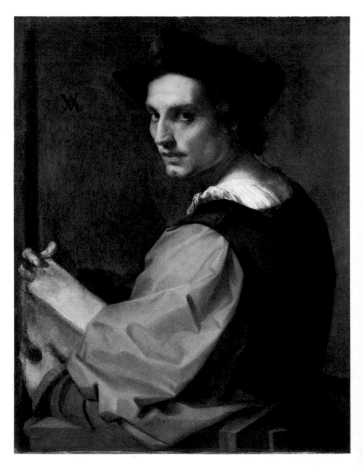

ANDREA D'AGNOLO called DEL SARTO
born and died Florence, 1486–1530
Portrait of a young man c 1517
canvas 72.4 × 57.2
signed with the artist's monogram
Purchased 1862

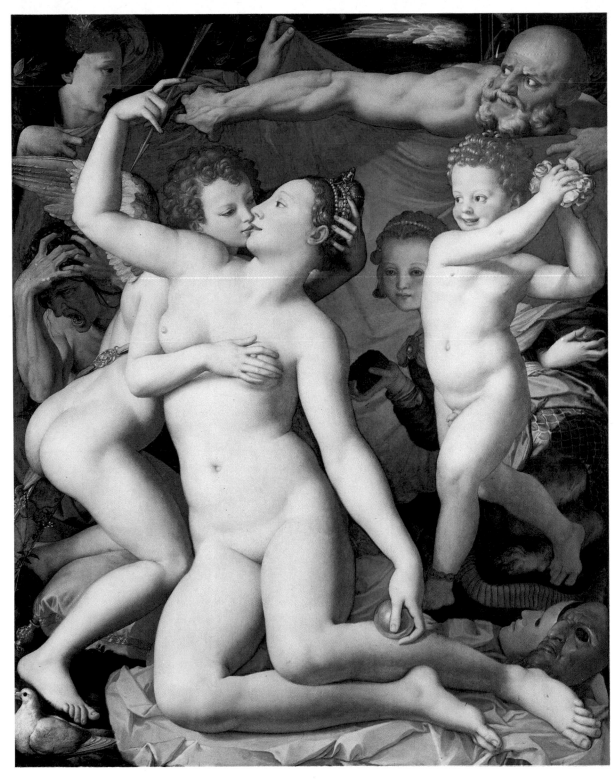

BRONZINO
born and died Florence, 1503–1572
An allegory probably 1540s or 1550s
wood 146.1 × 116.2
Purchased 1860

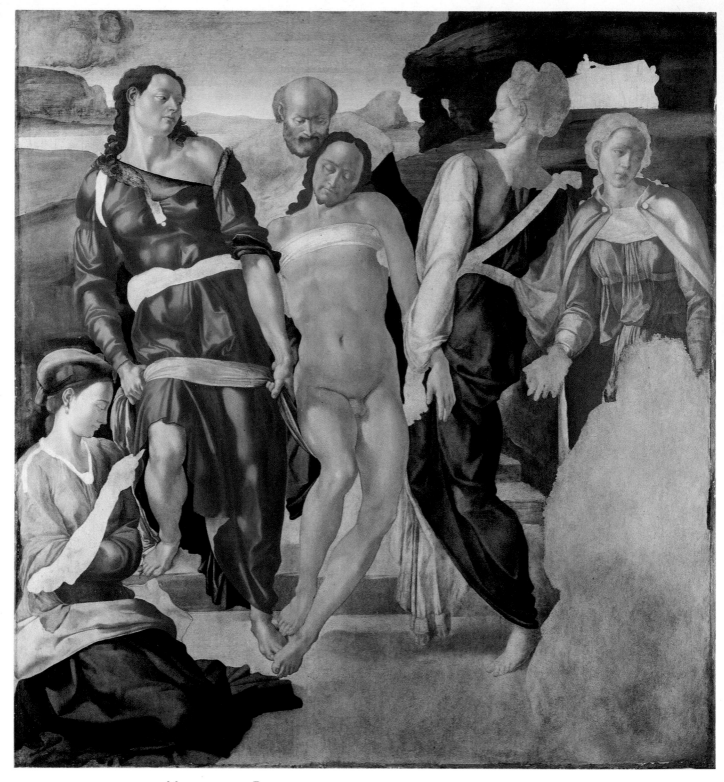

MICHELANGELO BUONARROTI
born Caprese 1475, died Rome 1564
The Entombment (unfinished)
   probably not earlier than 1505
wood 161.7 × 149.9
Purchased 1868

SEBASTIANO LUCIANI called SEBASTIANO DEL PIOMBO
born Venice c 1485, died Rome 1547
The Raising of Lazarus 1517/19
board, transferred from wood 381 × 289.6
signed
Purchased 1824

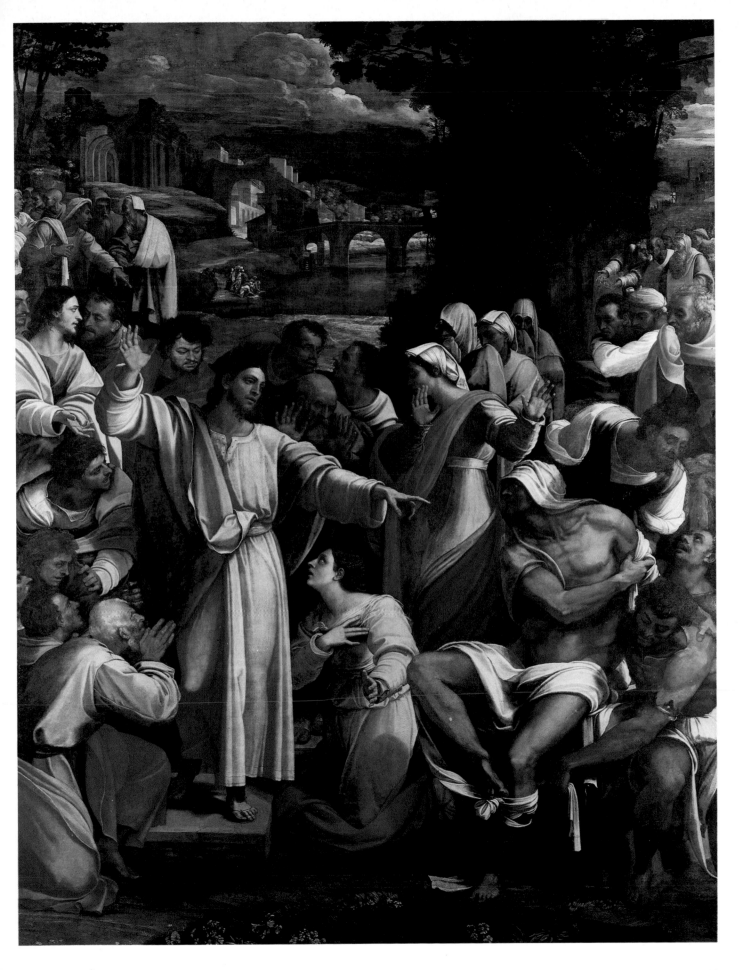

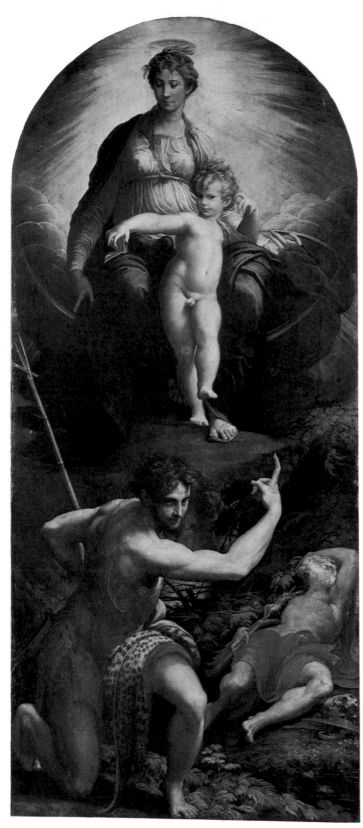

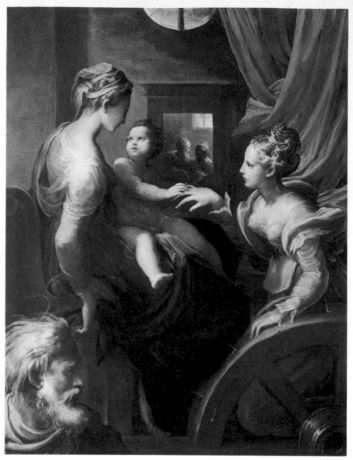

GIROLAMO FRANCESCO MARIA MAZZOLA called PARMIGIANINO
born and died Parma, 1503–1540
The Mystic Marriage of St Catherine
probably 1527/31
wood 74.2 × 57.2
Purchased 1974

JACOPO CARUCCI called PONTORMO
born Pontormo 1494, died Florence 1557
Joseph in Egypt (one of a series) c 1515
wood 96.5 × 109.5
Purchased 1882

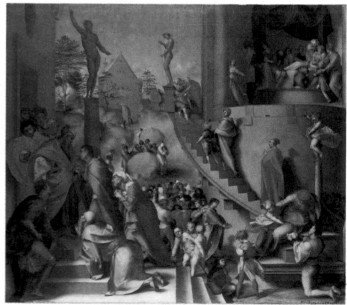

GIROLAMO FRANCESCO MARIA MAZZOLA called PARMIGIANINO
born and died Parma, 1503–1540
*Madonna and Child with St John the Baptist
  and St Jerome* (altarpiece) 1527
wood 342.9 × 148.6
Presented 1826

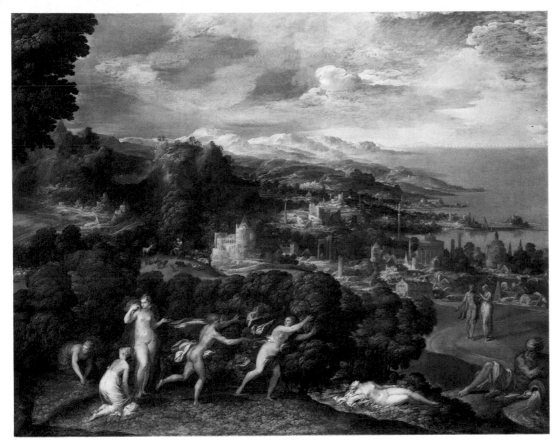

Ascribed to NICCOLO DELL
    'ABATE
born Modena c 1509/12,
    died Fontainebleau 1571
The story of Aristaeus after
    1552
canvas 189.2 × 237.5
Presented 1941

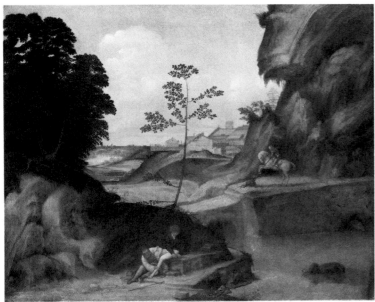

GIORGIO DA CASTELFRANCO called GIORGIONE
born Castelfranco 1477/78, died Venice 1510
Sunset landscape with saints, 'Il Tramonto'
    1504(?)
canvas 73.3 × 91.4
Purchased 1961

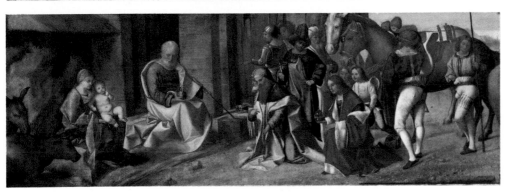

GIORGIO DA CASTELFRANCO called
    GIORGIONE
born Castelfranco 1477/78, died
    Venice 1510
The Adoration of the Magi 1506/07(?)
wood 29.8 × 81.3
Purchased 1884

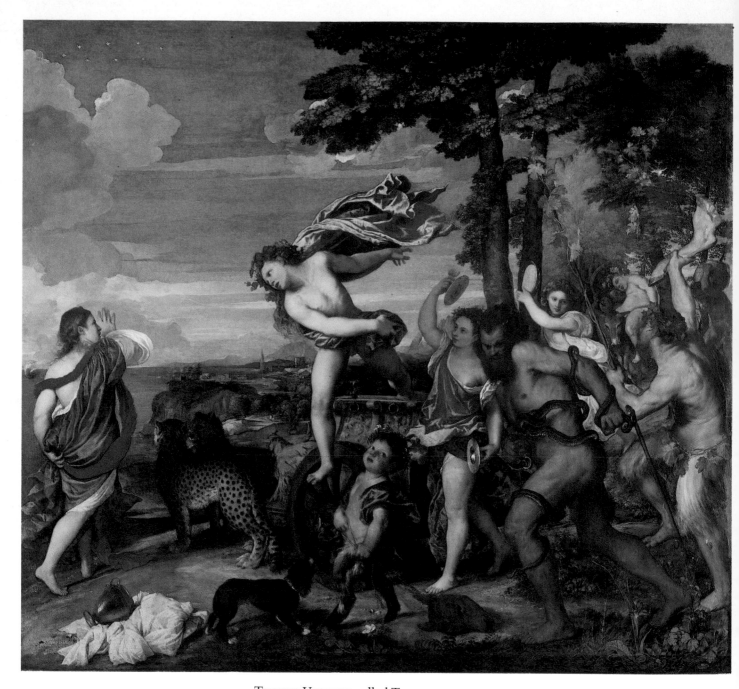

TIZIANO VECELLIO called TITIAN
born Pieve di Cadore c 1480, died Venice 1576
Bacchus and Ariadne 1523
canvas 175.2 × 190.5
signed
Purchased 1826

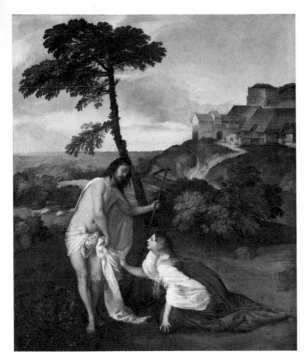

TIZIANO VECELLIO called TITIAN
born Pieve di Cadore c 1480, died Venice 1576
Noli me tangere an early work
canvas 108.6 × 90.8
Bequeathed 1856

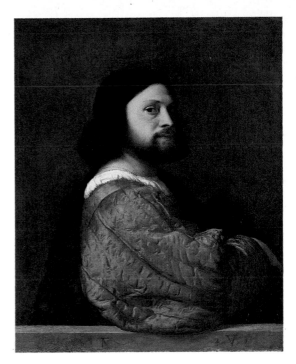

TIZIANO VECELLIO called TITIAN
born Pieve di Cadore c 1480, died Venice 1576
Portrait of a man c 1515(?)
canvas 81.2 × 66.3
Purchased 1904

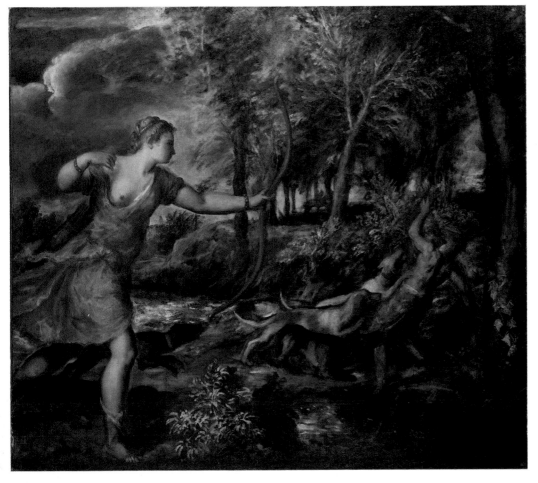

TIZIANO VECELLIO called TITIAN
born Pieve di Cadore c 1480,
    died Venice 1576
The death of Actaeon probably c 1559
canvas 178.4 × 198.1
Purchased 1972

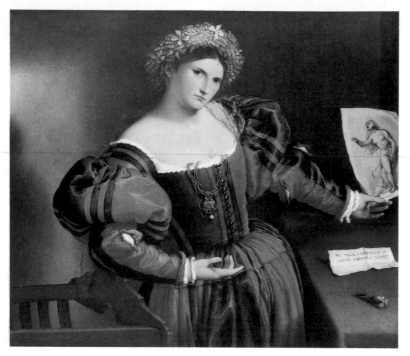

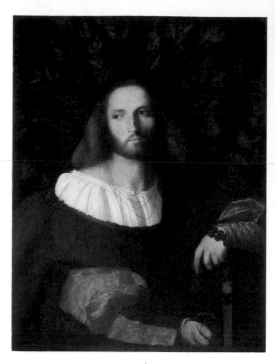

LORENZO LOTTO
born Venice c 1480, died Loreta after 1556
A lady as Lucretia c 1530
canvas 95.9 × 110.5
Inscribed in Latin: 'After Lucretia's example let no violated
      woman live.'
Purchased 1927

PALMA VECCHIO
born Bergamo c 1480, died Venice 1528
Portrait of a poet, probably Ariosto 1515/16(?)
wood 83.8 × 63.5
Purchased 1860

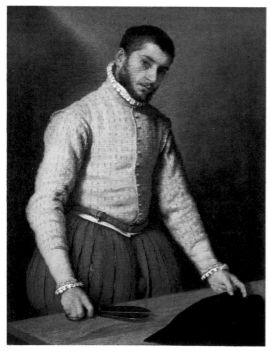

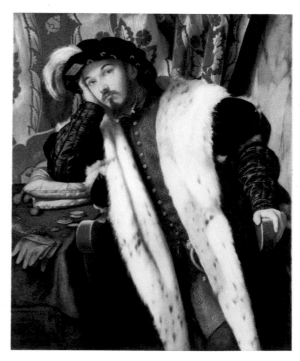

GIOVANNI BATTISTA MORONI
born Albino c 1525, died Bergamo 1578
Portrait of a man, 'The Tailor' c 1571
canvas 97.8 × 74.9
Purchased 1862

MORETTO DA BRESCIA
born and died Brescia, c 1498–1554
Portrait of a young man c mid 1530s/mid 1540s
canvas 113.7 × 94
Inscribed in Greek: 'Alas, I desire too much'
Purchased 1858

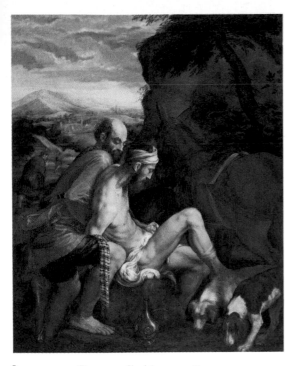

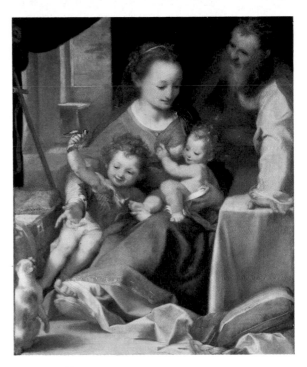

JACOPO DAL PONTE called JACOPO BASSANO
born and died Bassano, c 1510/18–1592
The Good Samaritan a middle period work
canvas 101.5 × 79.4
Purchased 1856

FEDERICO BAROCCI
born and died Urbino, 1535–1612
*Holy Family with the Infant Baptist, 'La Madonna del
  Gatto'* c 1577
canvas 112.7 × 92.7
Bequeathed 1831

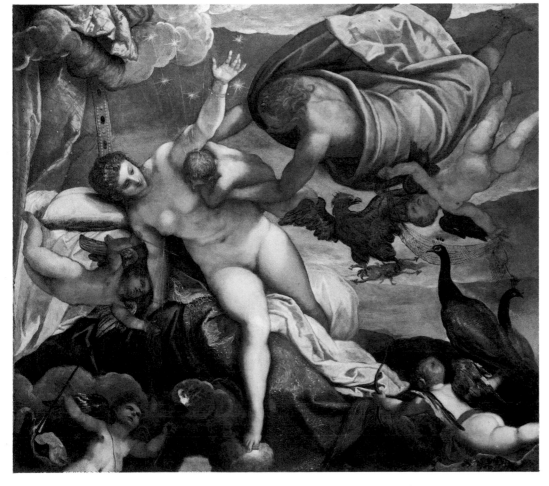

JACOPO ROBUSTI called
  TINTORETTO
born and died Venice, 1518–
  1594
The Origin of the Milky Way
  late 1570s(?)
canvas 148 × 165.1
Purchased 1890

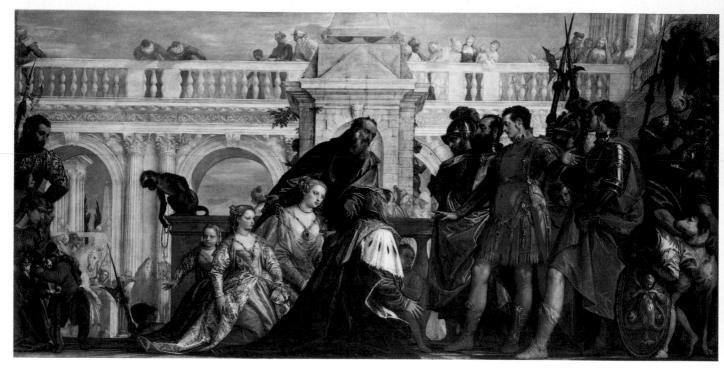

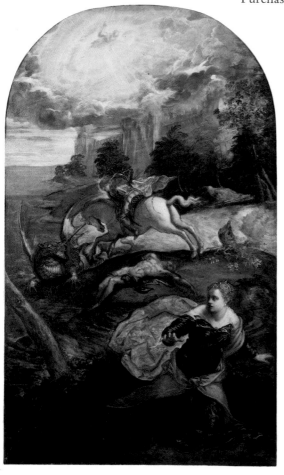

JACOPO ROBUSTI called TINTORETTO
born and died Venice, 1518–1594
St George and the Dragon 1560s(?)
canvas 157.5 × 100.3
Bequeathed 1831

PAOLO CALIARI called VERONESE
born Verona probably 1528, died
Venice 1588
The family of Darius before Alexander
late 1570s(?)
canvas 236.2 × 474.9
Purchased 1857

PAOLO CALIARI called VERONESE
born Verona probably 1528, died Venice 1588
The Vision of St Helena an early work(?)
canvas 197.5 × 115.6
Purchased 1878

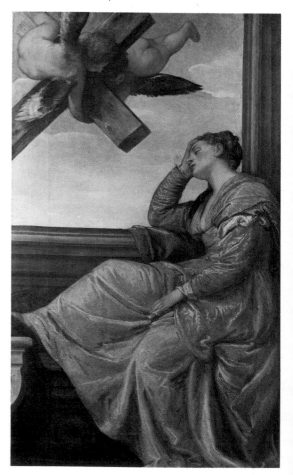

Seventeenth-century Holland and Flanders

The collection of seventeenth-century Dutch and Flemish painting is second only to the Italian collection in range and quality. The Gallery now has, for example, twenty-two works by Rembrandt and twenty-one by Rubens, although until the second half of the nineteenth century the Dutch School was very poorly represented. With only a few exceptions, Dutch artists were not amongst those collected by the English on a European Grand Tour in the eighteenth century, and the only Dutch pictures in the Angerstein collection were two by Rembrandt and Cuyp's *Hilly river landscape* (p 71). Among Holwell Carr's pictures was Rembrandt's *Woman bathing in a stream* (p 65) but critics bemoaned the absence of more characteristic representatives of the School, such as Hobbema and Ruisdael.

Rubens had been popular with English collectors throughout the eighteenth century and was from the first well represented in the Gallery. Since his visit to London in 1629/30 his influence on English artists had been strong; it is apparent particularly in the work of Gainsborough and Reynolds. Classicism, which was at no time so authoritative a movement in England as it was in France, never really threatened Rubens' reputation. '*Peace and War*' (p 76), which was presented to the Gallery in 1828 by the Duke of Sutherland, was painted in England as a present from Rubens to Charles I. It is an allegory of the diplomatic mission that brought him to England, showing Minerva (or Wisdom) defending Peace and her train against Mars (the god of War) and the destructive Furies.

Another Flemish painter with particular connections with England, who, like Rubens, was represented in Angerstein's collection, is Van Dyck. Charles I appointed him as his Court painter in 1632, and it was in London that he died. One of the Gallery's largest pictures is the *Equestrian portrait of Charles I* (p 83), executed for the King towards the end of the 1630s and purchased in 1885. The landscape background and loose painterly handling established the format for British portraiture until the end of the nineteenth century.

Virtually every aspect of the work of both Rubens and Van Dyck is now represented at the National Gallery. The *Autumn landscape* (p 80), which formed part of Sir George Beaumont's gift and shows Rubens' own house, is the chief of a number of fine landscapes, which are later echoed in Gainsborough's *Watering place* (p 117). The *Woman and child* (p 81) illustrates the virtuosity of Van Dyck's early portrait style while he was still living at Antwerp. In addition to the Portrait of Charles I, a recently acquired double portrait of *Lady Elizabeth Thimbleby and Dorothy, Viscountess Andover* (p 82) well represents the opulence of his English period. Another recent acquisition, Rubens' *Samson and Delilah* (p 79), has significantly augmented the Gallery's collection of the artist's work. This immensely powerful and dramatic painting, executed in about 1610/12, was purchased at auction in 1980 for over £2 million and shows the enormous ability of the young painter on his return from Italy, when he was still strongly under the influence of Caravaggio. Rubens' pupil Jacob Jordaens is represented by both religious works and the superb double portrait of *Govaert van Surpele and his wife* (p 84), purchased in 1958.

It was only in the nineteenth century that many Dutch artists, the realistic painters of northern landscape like Ruisdael and Hobbema (as opposed to the Italianate landscapists such as Both and Berchem whose popularity dates from the eighteenth century), began to be appreciated in England. Their fidelity to nature and the absence of idealisation in their works, coupled with their detailed finish, appealed to a new type of collector of the professional or merchant classes who began to play a significant role as arbiters of taste in this century. Sir Robert Peel, who played such a large part in the Gallery's early history, came from a wealthy manufacturing family and built one of the most notable collections of Dutch pictures in the country during the first half of the century. Mrs Anne Jameson, herself an enthusiast for such painting, described Peel's collection in her *Private Galleries of Art in London* of 1844 as 'the most remarkable and valuable collection with which I am acquainted'.

It was this collection that formed the basis of the Dutch collection at the National Gallery. Seventy-seven pictures, fifty-five of them Dutch, and eighteen drawings were bought in 1871 from the Peel collection for a total of £75,000. They included Hobbema's masterpiece *The Avenue, Middelharnis* (p 76), two fine de Hooghs, an *Interior* and *The courtyard of a house* (p 75), Metsu's *Man and woman beside a virginal* (p 73) and Rubens' famous '*Le Chapeau de Paille*' (p 82), a portrait of his wife's sister Susanna Fourment.

Five years later Wynn Ellis, a silk manufacturer and Free Trade Liberal, left his collection of 403 pictures to the Gallery. Ninety-four were selected and the rest sold. The majority were once again Dutch and show the collector's preference for realistic 'well-made' pictures. They include works by Ruisdael, for example his *Landscape with a ruined castle and a church* (p 76), van de Cappelle, van de Velde and van der Heyden, and Berchem's *A man and Youth ploughing* (p 70), which had once belonged to the French painter Boucher.

In 1910 the third considerable group of Dutch pictures came to the Gallery as part of the bequest of George Salting, which included fine works of most schools. The *Young woman seated at a virginal* (p 73), the second and last painting by Vermeer to be acquired, was the most important work in this collection. It joined the *Young woman standing at a virginal* (p 74) already in the Gallery, and the two paintings may indeed be a pair representing sacred and profane love. They had both formerly belonged to the critic and writer Théophile Thoré, whose articles in the *Gazette des Beaux-Arts* in 1866 had led to a renewed appreciation of this rare artist. Among the remaining works in Salting's collection were paintings by Cuyp, Metsu, Jan Steen, Ruisdael and Frans Hals (including his *Portrait of a man* (p 65)) and Saenredam's interior of *The Grote Kerk, Haarlem* (p 69).

Unlike other Dutch artists, Rembrandt has always been admired and appreciated, and throughout its history the Gallery has acquired major examples of his work. Today Rembrandt's enormous range is well represented. The religious works include episodes from the life of Christ and the large and dramatic Old Testament scene, *Belshazzar's Feast* (p 69). Among outstanding examples of his portraiture are a late portrait of the merchant Jacob Trip, and two contemporaneous portraits of Trip's wife, *Margaretha de Geer* (p 68), which convey with great power and compassion the frailty of the elderly lady. The Gallery also owns two of Rembrandt's numerous self-portraits, a highly self-conscious one of 1640, which was perhaps painted in emulation of Titian's *Portrait of a man* (p 57), and another painted some thirty years later shortly before his death.

The Gallery has continued to buy major works by Dutch and Flemish artists, many of them by private treaty arrangement from British owners. Since no tax is payable on such sales, both owner and Gallery benefit financially, and important paintings are thereby preserved for the nation. Among the works acquired in this way in recent years are Koninck's *Extensive landscape* (p 71), Rembrandt's portrait of his mistress *Hendrickje Stoffels* (p 67), the double portrait of *Lady Elizabeth Thimbleby and Dorothy, Viscountess Andover* by Van Dyck and the brilliant *Young Man holding a skull* (p 66) by Frans Hals.

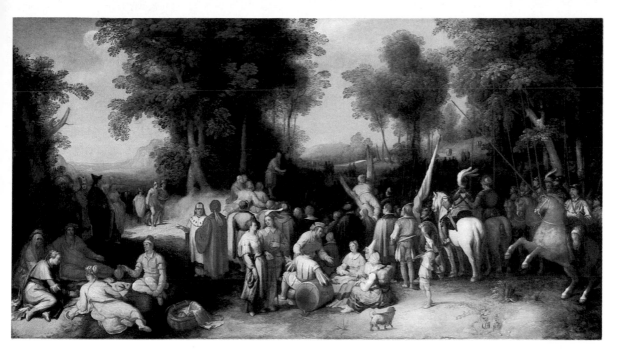

CORNELIS VAN HAARLEM
born and died Haarlem, 1562–1638
The preaching of St John the Baptist 1602
canvas 100 × 180
signed and dated
Purchased 1978

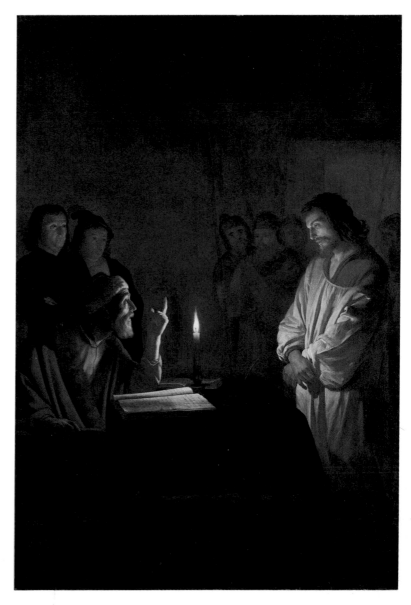

GERRIT VAN HONTHORST
born and died Utrecht, 1590–1656
Christ before the High Priest c 1617(?)
canvas 269.2 × 182.9
Purchased 1922

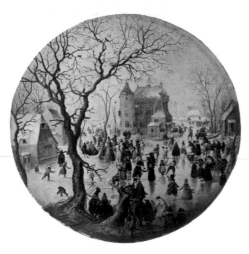

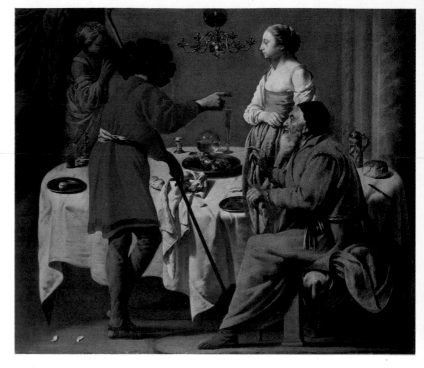

HENDRICK AVERCAMP
born Amsterdam 1585, died Kampen 1634
A winter scene with skaters near a castle an
   early work
wood diameter 40.7
signed
Purchased 1891

HENDRICK TER BRUGGHEN
born 1588(?), died Utrecht 1629
Jacob reproaching Laban 1627
canvas 97.5 × 114.3
signed and dated
Purchased 1926

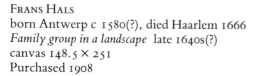

FRANS HALS
born Antwerp c 1580(?), died Haarlem 1666
Family group in a landscape late 1640s(?)
canvas 148.5 × 251
Purchased 1908

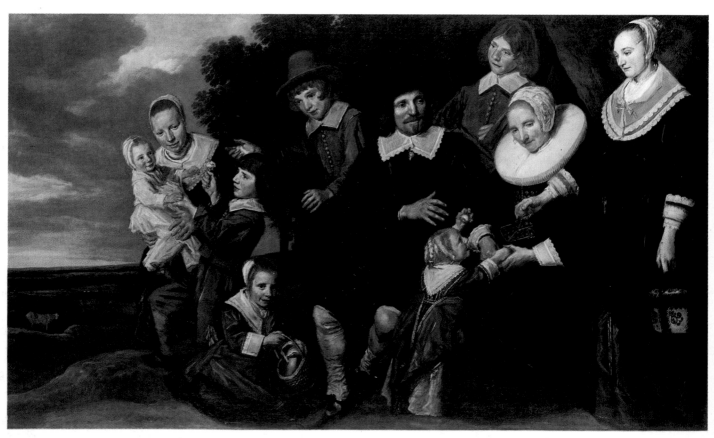

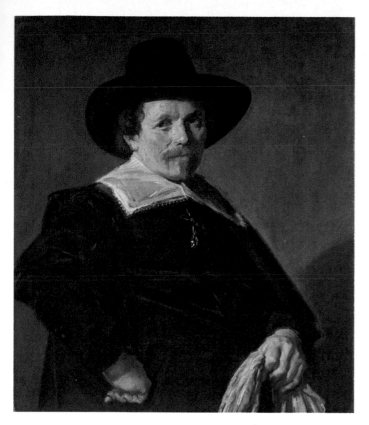

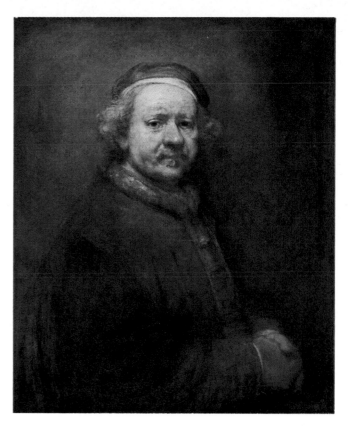

FRANS HALS
born Antwerp c 1580(?), died Haarlem 1666
Portrait of a man mid 1640s(?)
canvas 78. 5 × 67.3
Bequeathed 1910

REMBRANDT HARMENSZ VAN RIJN
born Leyden 1606, died Amsterdam 1669
Self-portrait aged sixty-three 1669
canvas 86 × 70. 5
remains of a signature and dated
Purchased 1851

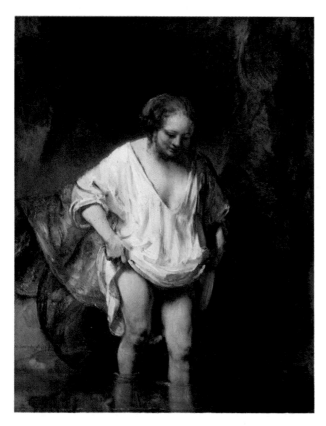

REMBRANDT HARMENSZ VAN RIJN
born Leyden 1606, died Amsterdam 1669
Woman bathing in a stream 1655
wood 61.8 × 47
signed and dated
Bequeathed 1831

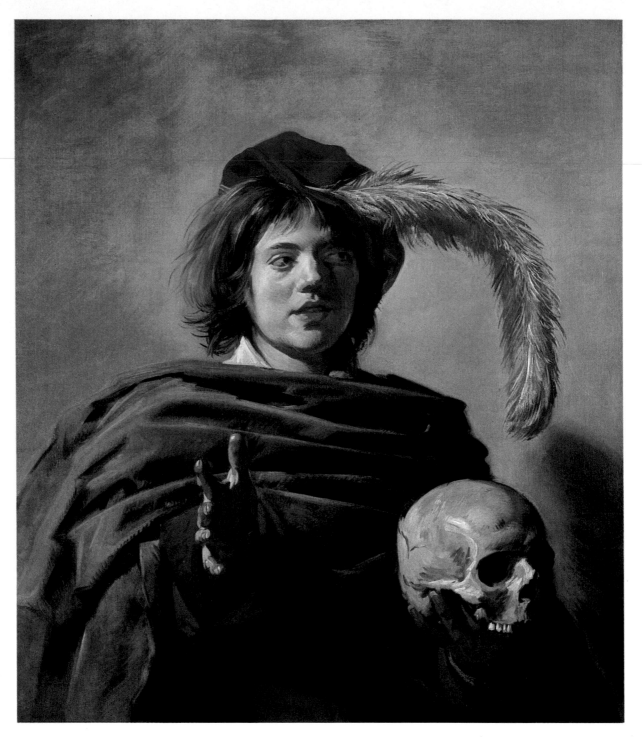

FRANS HALS
born Antwerp c 1580(?), died Haarlem 1666
Young Man holding a skull c 1626
canvas 92 × 81
Purchased 1980

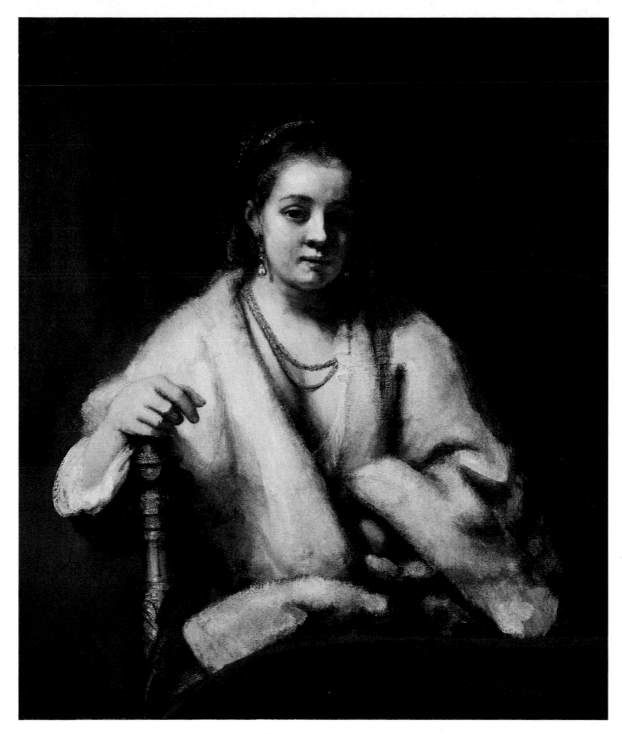

REMBRANDT HARMENSZ VAN RIJN
born Leyden 1606, died Amsterdam 1669
Hendrickje Stoffels 1659
canvas 101.9 × 83.75
signed and dated
Purchased 1976

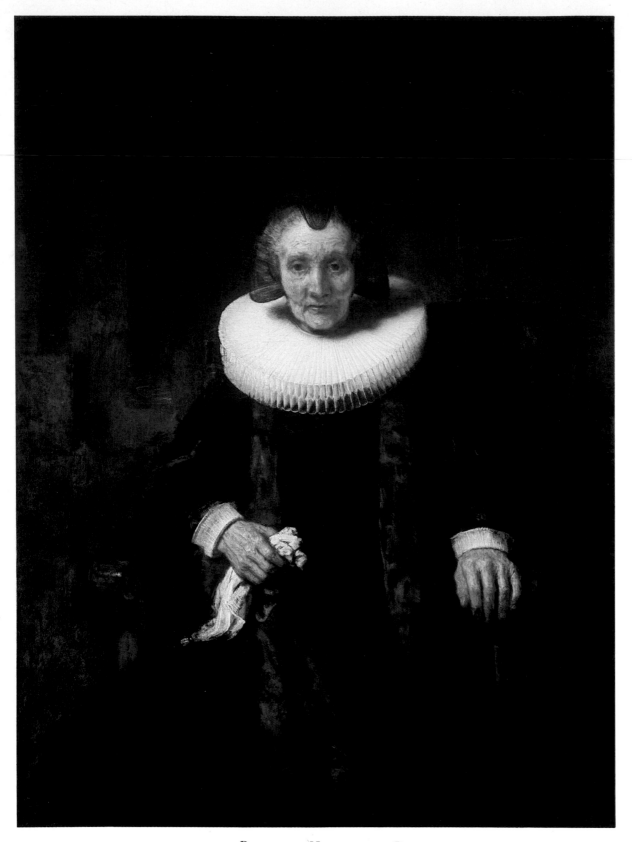

Rembrandt Harmensz van Rijn
born Leyden 1606, died Amsterdam 1669
Margaretha de Geer c 1661
canvas 130.5 × 97.5
Purchased 1851

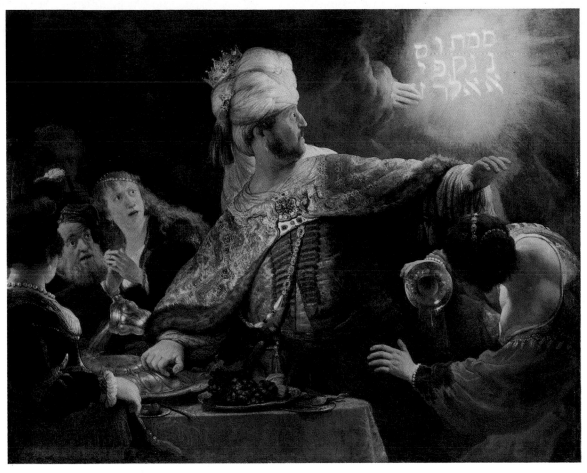

REMBRANDT HARMENSZ
  VAN RIJN
born Leyden 1606, died
  Amsterdam 1669
Belshazzar's Feast 163(?)
canvas 167.6 × 209.2
signed and dated
Purchased 1964

PIETER SAENREDAM
born Assendelft 1597, died Haarlem 1665
The Grote Kerk, Haarlem 1636/37
wood 59.5 × 81.7
Bequeathed 1910

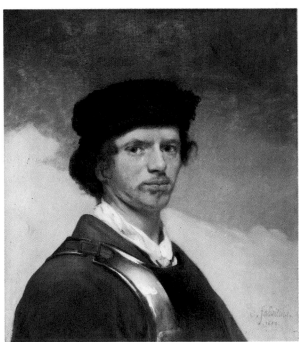

CAREL FABRITIUS
born Midden-Beemster 1622, died Delft 1654
Self-portrait 1654
canvas 70.5 × 61.6
signed and dated
Purchased 1924

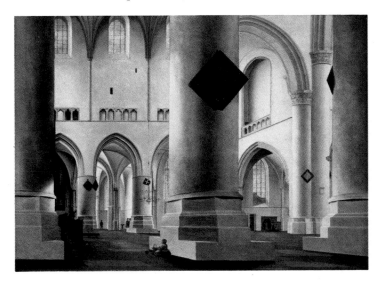

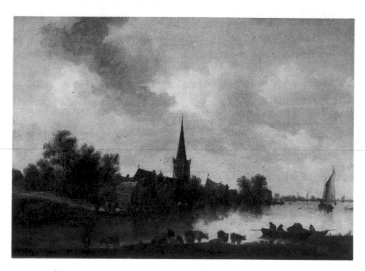

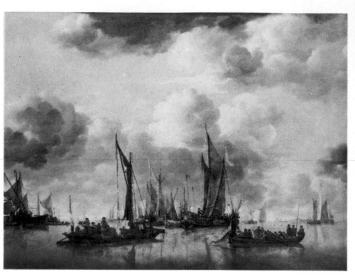

JAN VAN GOYEN
born Leyden 1596, died The Hague 1656
A view of Overschie 1645
wood 66 × 96.5
signed and dated
Bequeathed 1852

JAN VAN DE CAPPELLE
born and died Amsterdam, c 1623/25–1679
A shipping scene with a Dutch yacht firing a salute 1650
wood 85.5 × 114.5
signed and dated
Bequeathed 1876

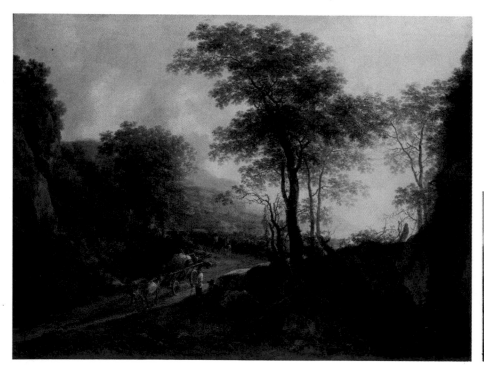

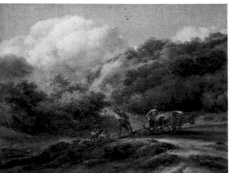

JAN BOTH
born and died Utrecht, c 1618(?)–1652
A rocky landscape with an ox-cart
canvas 120.5 × 160.5
signed
Bequeathed 1902

NICOLAES BERCHEM
born Haarlem 1620, died
    Amsterdam 1683
A man and youth ploughing 1658
canvas 38.2 × 51.5
signed
Bequeathed 1876

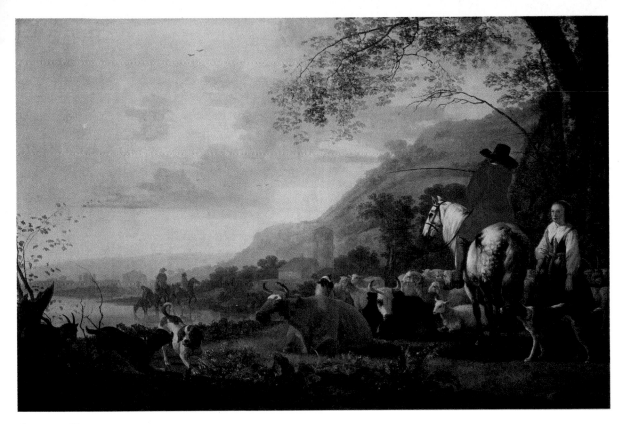

AELBERT CUYP
born and died Dordrecht, 1620–1691
A hilly river landscape c 1655–66(?)
canvas 135.2 × 200
signed
Purchased 1824

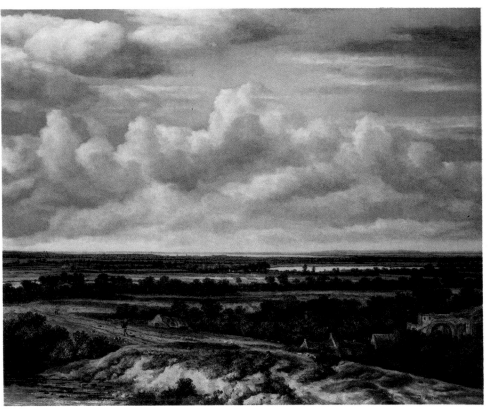

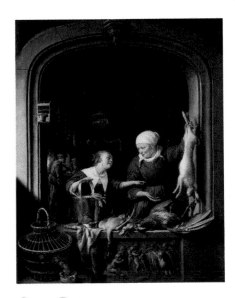

GERRIT DOU
born and died Leyden, 1613–1675
A poulterer's shop a late work(?)
wood 58 × 46
signed
Purchased 1871

PHILIPS KONINCK
born and died Amsterdam, 1619–1688
Extensive landscape with a road by a ruin 1655
canvas 137.4 × 167.7
signed and dated
Purchased 1971

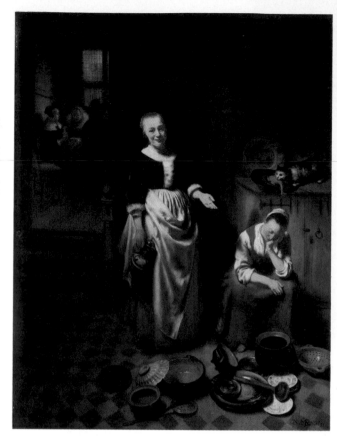

NICOLAES MAES
born Dordrecht 1634, died Amsterdam 1693
Sleeping maid and her servant 1655
wood 70 × 53.3
signed and dated
Bequeathed 1847

JAN STEEN
born and died Leyden, 1625/6–1679
The effects of intemperance
wood 76 × 106.5
signed
Purchased 1977

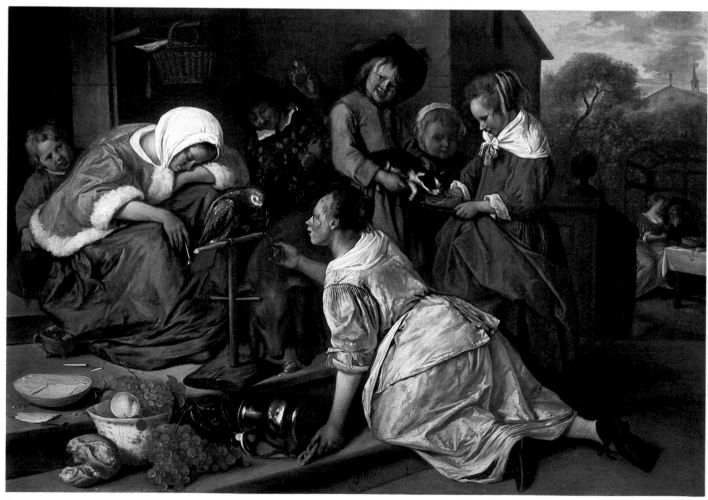

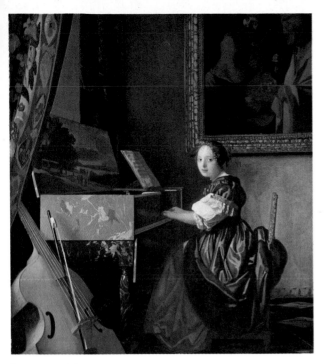

JOHANNES VERMEER
born and died Delft, 1632–1675
Young woman seated at a virginal probably late 1670s
canvas 51.5 × 45.5
signed
Bequeathed 1910

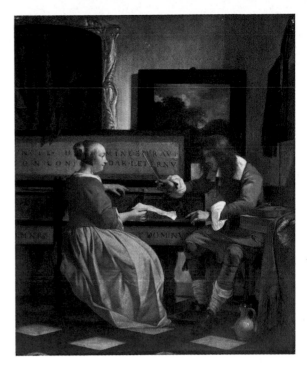

GABRIEL METSU
born Leyden 1629, died Amsterdam 1677
A man and woman beside a virginal probably late 1650s
wood 38.4 × 32.2
Inscribed on the virginal from the Psalms (Vulgate:
 XXX.2, and LXX.1; cl.6)
signed
Purchased 1871

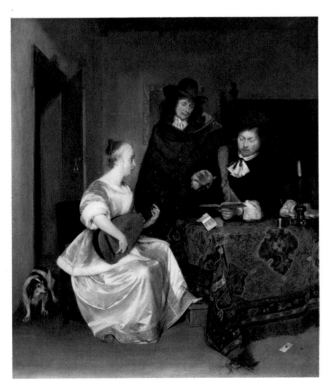

GERARD TER BORCH
born Zwolle 1617, died Deventer 1681
A woman making music with two men probably c 1670
canvas 67.6 × 57.8
Purchased 1871

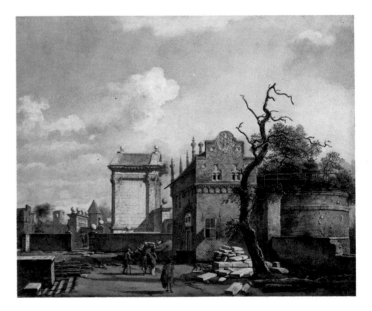

JAN VAN DER HEYDEN
born Gorinchem 1637, died Amsterdam 1712
An architectural fantasy late 1660s(?)
wood 51.8 × 64.5
signed
Bequeathed 1876

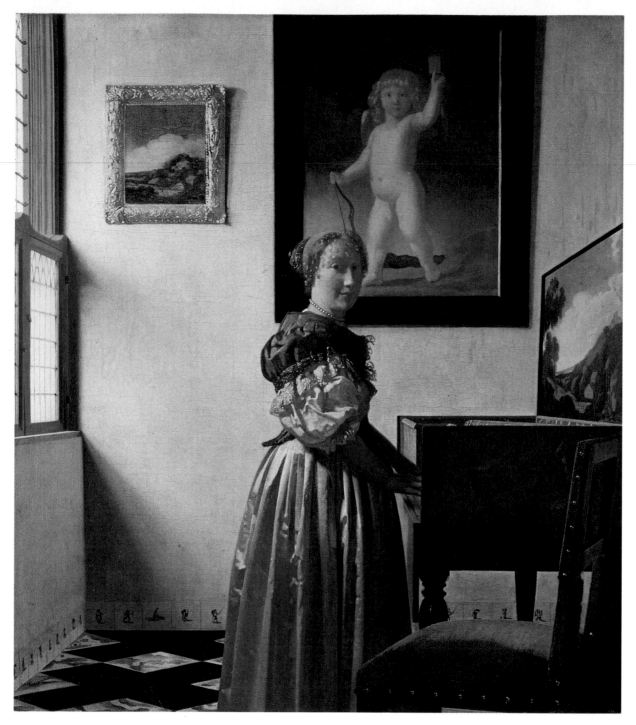

JOHANNES VERMEER
born and died Delft, 1632–1675
Young woman standing at a virginal c 1670
canvas 51.7 × 45.2
signed
Purchased 1892

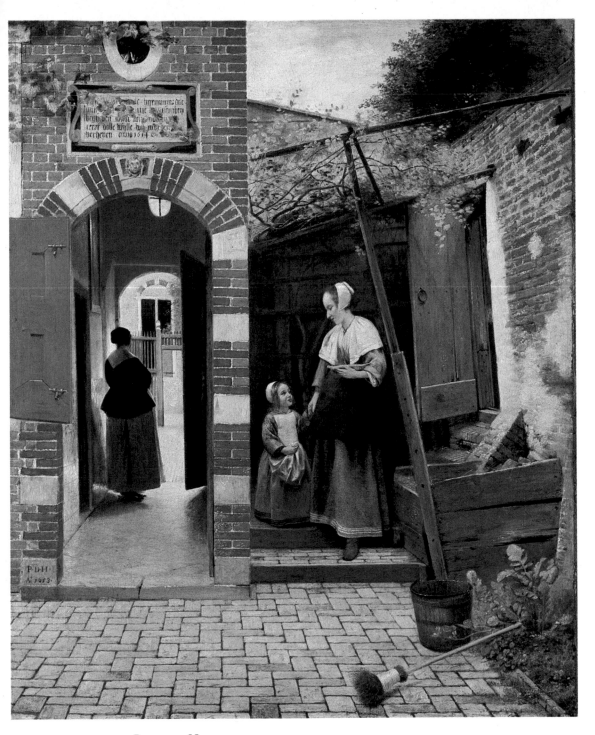

PIETER DE HOOGH
born Rotterdam 1629, died Amsterdam after 1684(?)
The courtyard of a house in Delft 1658
canvas 73.5 × 60
signed and dated
Purchased 1871

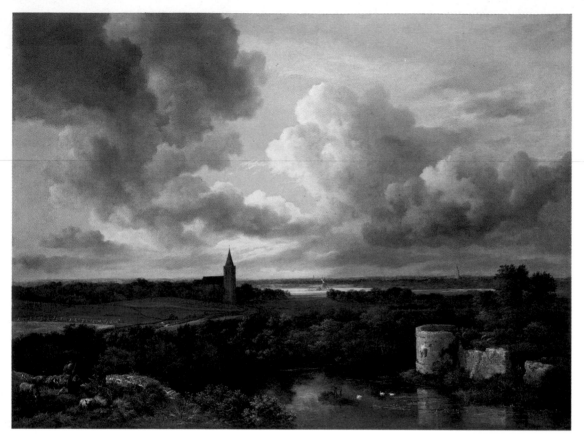

Jacob van Ruisdael
born and died Haarlem, 1628/29–1682
Landscape with a ruined castle and a church late 1660s
canvas 109.2 × 146.1
signed
Bequeathed 1876

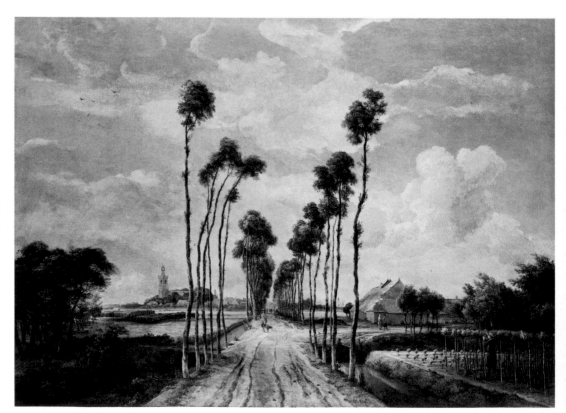

Meyndert Hobbema
born and died
Amsterdam, 1638–1709
The Avenue, Middelharnis
1689
canvas 103.5 × 141
signed and dated
Purchased 1871

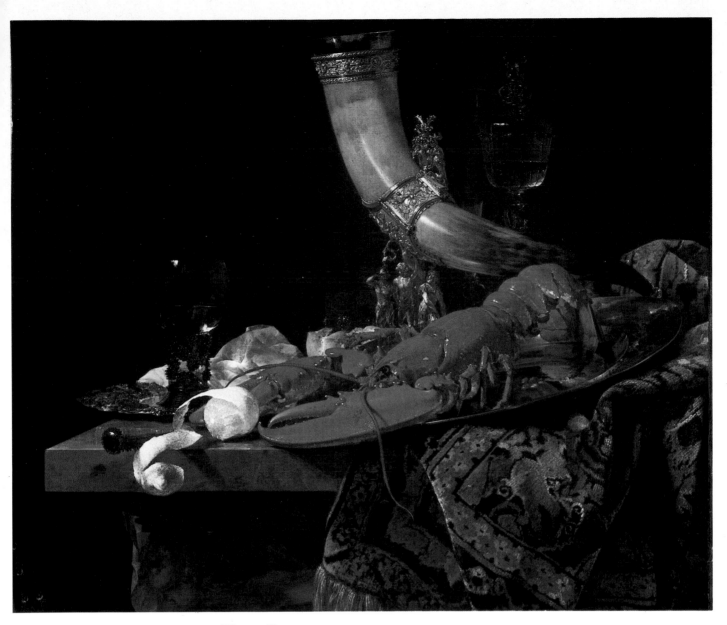

WILLEM KALF
born and died Amsterdam, 1619–1693
*Still-life with the drinking-horn of the St Sebastian Archers' Guild, a
    lobster and glasses* c 1653
canvas 86.4 × 102.2
signed
Bequeathed 1978

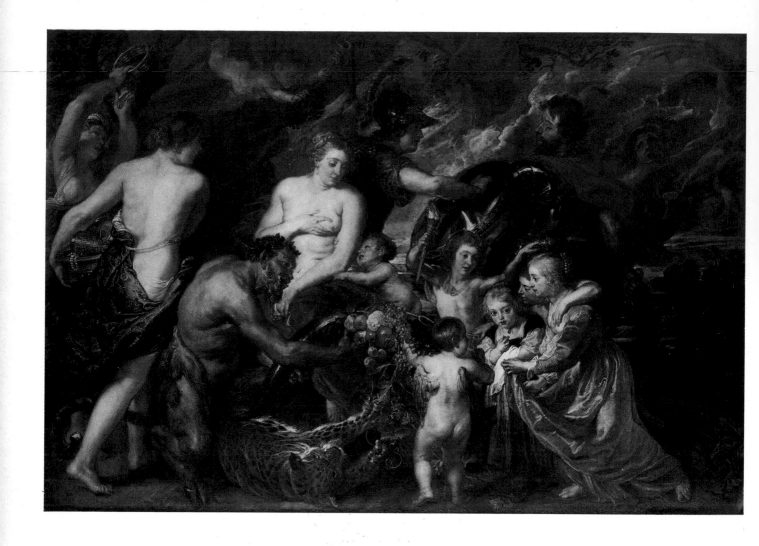

PEETER PAUWEL RUBENS
born Siegen 1577, died Antwerp 1640
Minerva protects Pax from Mars, 'Peace and War' 1629/30
canvas 203.5 × 298
Presented 1828

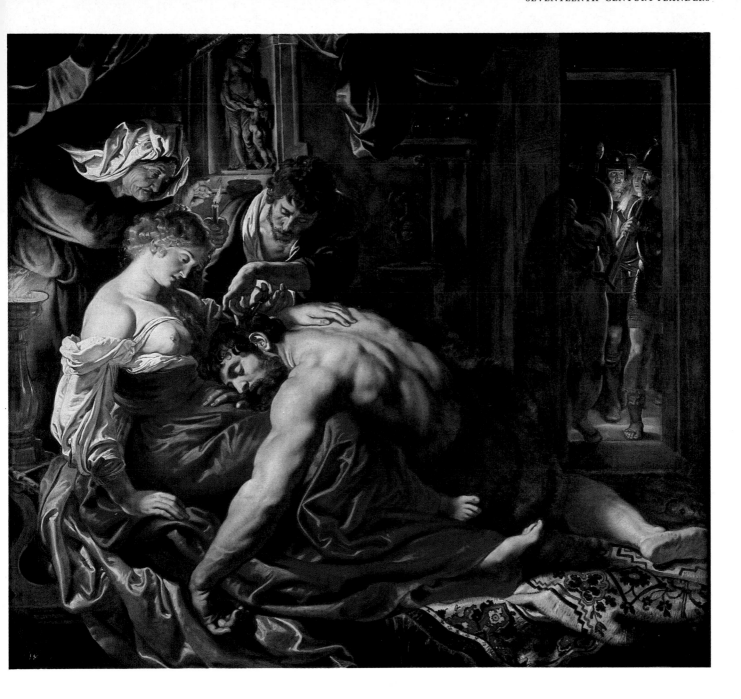

PEETER PAUWEL RUBENS
born Siegen 1577, died Antwerp 1640
Samson and Delilah c 1610/12
wood 185 × 205
Purchased 1980

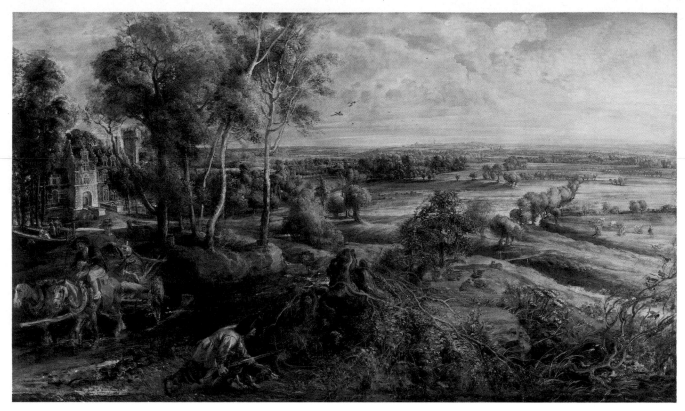

PEETER PAUWEL RUBENS
born Siegen 1577, died Antwerp 1640
Autumn landscape with a view of Het Steen 1636
wood 131.2 × 229.2
Presented 1823/28

PEETER PAUWEL RUBENS
born Siegen 1577, died Antwerp 1640
The Judgement of Paris probably c 1632/35
wood 144.8 × 193.7
Purchased 1844

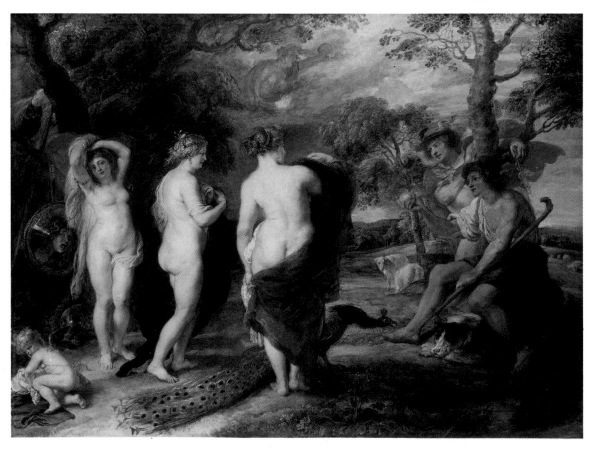

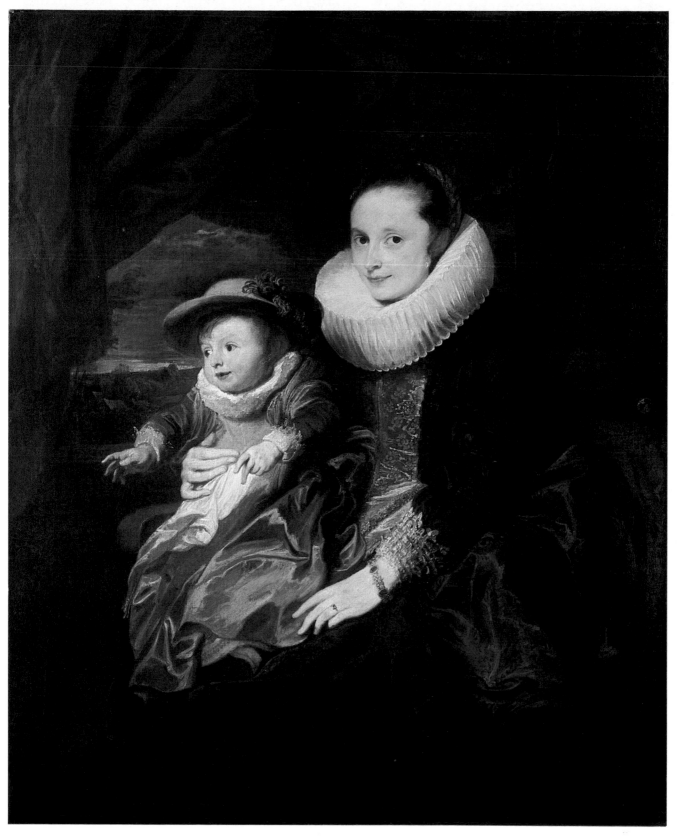

ANTHONY VAN DYCK
born Antwerp 1599, died London 1641
A woman and child 1620/21
canvas 131.5 × 106.2
Purchased 1914

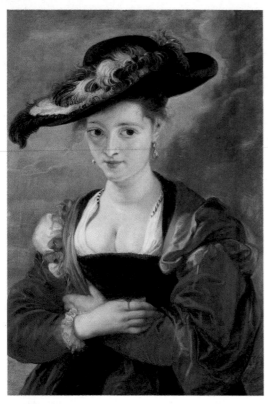

PEETER PAUWEL RUBENS
born Siegen 1577, died Antwerp 1640
Susanna Lunden, 'Le Chapeau de Paille'
c 1622/25
wood 79 × 54
Purchased 1871

ANTHONY VAN DYCK
born Antwerp 1599, died London 1641
Lady Elizabeth Thimbleby and Dorothy, Viscountess Andover
  c 1637
canvas 132 × 149.5
Purchased 1977

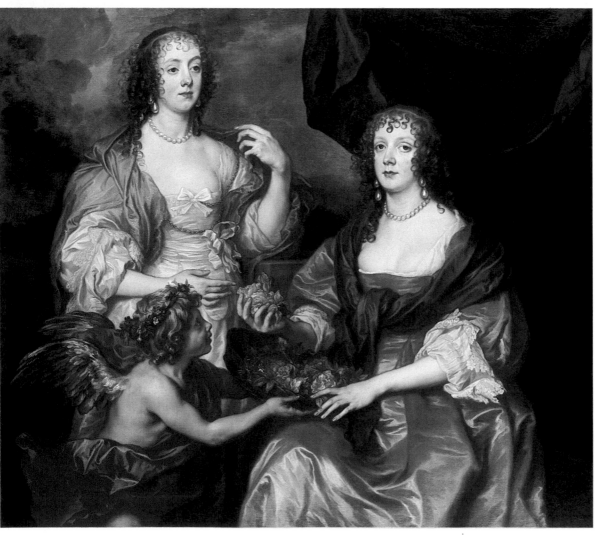

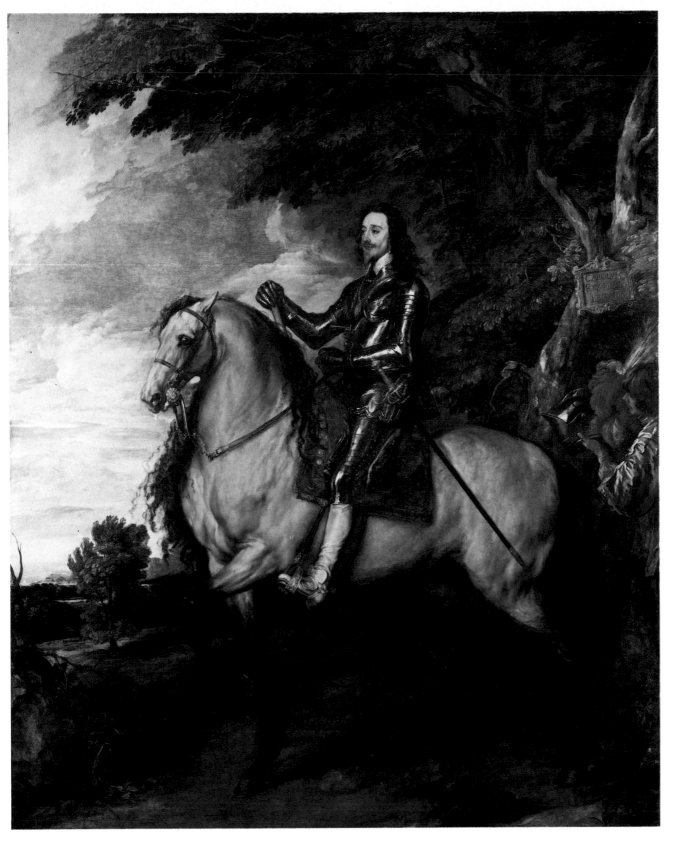

ANTHONY VAN DYCK
born Antwerp 1599, died London 1641
Equestrian portrait of Charles I probably late 1630s
canvas 367 × 292.1
Inscribed: CAROLVS/REX MAGNAE/BRITANIAE
Purchased 1885

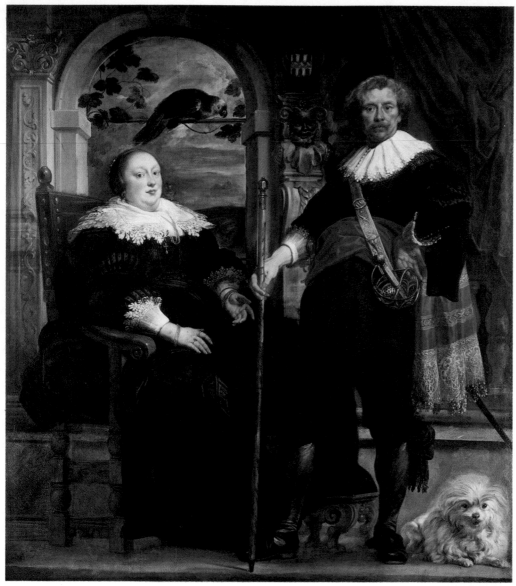

JACOB JORDAENS
born and died Antwerp, 1593–
1678
Govaert van Surpele and his wife
c 1630/35(?)
canvas 213.4 × 188.9
Purchased 1958

JACOB VAN OOST I
born and died Bruges, 1601–1671
A boy aged eleven 1650
canvas 80.5 × 63
signed and dated
Purchased 1883

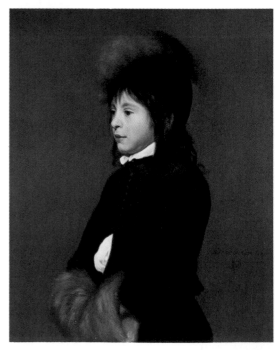

Seventeenth-century Italy, France and Spain

The seventeenth-century Bolognese painters, Guercino, Domenichino, Guido Reni and the Carracci, enjoyed a popularity among English collectors of the eighteenth century that is difficult to conceive today. There are still fine examples of their work in many private collections in this country, but their names are now comparatively little known. They have long been held in poor favour and many of the Gallery's examples of their work were acquired early in its history, in the first half of the nineteenth century.

There were examples by these artists or their contemporaries among both the Angerstein and Holwell Carr pictures, and in 1836 William IV himself presented two large mythological works which probably derive from the studio of Guido Reni. A very fine Annibale Carracci showing *Christ appearing to St Peter on the Appian Way* (p 88) was purchased in 1826, and in the 1840s began a whole spate of purchases of the works of Bolognese painters. One of the finest of these was the *Lot and his daughters* (p 90) by Guido Reni, but others were later found to be copies or poor studio versions. It was these unwise purchases together with the scandal over the cleaning of pictures that led to the Inquiry of 1853 and finally in 1855 to the revision of the Gallery's constitution.

But the attack upon the Gallery's policy of acquisition, in which Ruskin occupied a front-line position, ought to be seen in the wider context of the rediscovery of the 'primitives' of both Italy and the north and the concomitant devaluation of seventeenth and eighteenth century painting. In the view of serious minds, Reni and Boucher were damned alike for their artificiality and lack of moral intention. A cloud of disrepute has since hung over the Bolognese painters, and the word 'eclectic' is used of them in a derogatory sense, implying an absence of originality. Although the qualities of these artists are not as immediately apparent as those of Caravaggio, a contemporary artist working further south in Italy, there is a fine sense of drama in both Annibale Carracci's '*The Three Maries*' (p 89) and Guercino's *Incredulity of St Thomas* (p 90). Differences of character are conveyed by the subtly varied poses and gestures, which are also designed to cohere in a formally satisfying composition. Caravaggio's unmistakable brand of realism is, on the other hand, arresting and aggresively dramatic, with strong contrasts of light and shade, as seen in his *Supper at Emmaus* (p 87).

Many foreign artists who trained in Italy carried Caravaggio's influence all over Europe. In Germany, we find in the works of Elsheimer a new application of his light effects in very small and delicate paintings (p 89). In Naples, which in the seventeenth century was under Spanish possession, a whole generation of Italian and Spanish artists, including Giordano (p 91) and Ribera (p 102), adopted a style based on his work, and Velázquez was already showing Caravaggio's influence in such works as the *Kitchen scene* (p 98) before his visit to Italy in 1629/31. Among French artists too he had his followers. In *The Four Ages of Man* (p 90) by Le Valentin, who was working in Rome in the 1620s, the raking light and chiaroscuro are derived from Caravaggio.

Claude and Poussin, the two most famous French artists of the century, both settled in Rome and died there. Claude is commonly regarded as the originator of the 'classical landscape', but while he refined it and made it popular, Domenichino had already painted many pictures in which landscape played the chief part. Examples such as *Tobias and the Angel* (p 89) illustrate his preference for subjects which can be treated with figures subordinated to landscape. Although Claude also painted religious subjects, many of his landscapes depict incidents from classical history or mythology. In *Cephalus and Procris* (p 97), the real landscape around Rome is combined with buildings and vistas of an imagined golden age, which demonstrates one reason for the enormous popularity of Claude's paintings with English collectors in the eighteenth century. At a time when the gentry were cultivating a taste for things classical and for building villas in the Palladian style, his work proposed a vision of the landscape of the classical past which was imitated in countless parks and gardens.

Among Angerstein's pictures were five Claudes. Four more formed part of Sir George

Beaumont's gift, although the *Hagar and the Angel* (p 95), to which of all his pictures he was most attached, did not enter the collection until after his death in 1828. John Constable, a friend of Beaumont, copied this work and its influence can still be felt in *The Haywain* (p 126). In the eighteenth century and later, Claude, Poussin and Poussin's brother-in-law, Gaspard Dughet (several examples of whose work were among the Angerstein and Holwell Carr pictures), were much imitated by English landscape painters. Turner in his early work produced virtual pastiches of all three. Meanwhile it was Salvator Rosa (p 91) who provided a model for 'sublime' landscape and who, with his intensely dramatic treatment and irregular, rugged outlines particularly appealed to the romantic sensibility at the end of the eighteenth century.

The first Spanish artist to be represented in the National Gallery was Murillo, who for most of the nineteenth century was probably also the most popular. His *Peasant boy leaning on a sill* (p 99) was presented to the Gallery in 1826 and the large canvas of *The Two Trinities* (p 102) was bought in 1837. Velázquez's *Boar Hunt*, purchased in 1846, was the first of his works to be acquired, and the stunning full-length portrait of *Philip IV of Spain* (p 101) was purchased by Burton in 1882. El Greco, however, was little known until the end of the century. In 1895 the Gallery bought *Christ driving the traders from the Temple* (p 100), which shows well his arresting style in which High Renaissance motifs, derived from Michelangelo, Titian and Tintoretto, are moulded into a totally personal idiom.

One of the greatest Spanish works in the collection and the only surviving nude by Velázquez, '*The Rokeby Venus*' (p 98), was presented to the Gallery in 1906 by the National Art-Collections Fund. This famous picture, which had hung at Rokeby Park in Yorkshire for almost one hundred years, is painted with loose brush strokes and shows Velázquez freely improvising on the traditional theme of Venus at her mirror. It was the first major work of art to be saved by the Fund which raised £45,000 to acquire it. Soon after its arrival at Trafalgar Square the picture was the subject of a violent attack by a suffragette, and was slashed by a knife – a wry testimony to the enduring power of Velázquez's image. Another serious act of vandalism was committed in 1978 when Poussin's *Adoration of the Golden Calf* (p 96) was attacked and torn from its frame. Like '*The Rokeby Venus*', Poussin's large biblical composition has been painstakingly restored, with the pieces of canvas laid down on a board and all damage skilfully touched out, so that although no longer intact, the painting is preserved and the image unimpaired.

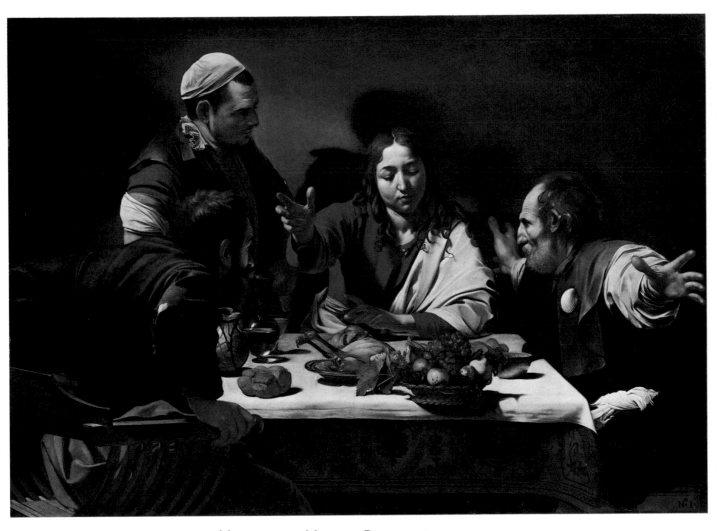

MICHELANGELO MERISI DA CARAVAGGIO
born Caravaggio 1573, died Porto Ercole 1610
The Supper at Emmaus c 1596/1602(?)
canvas 141 × 196.2
Presented 1839

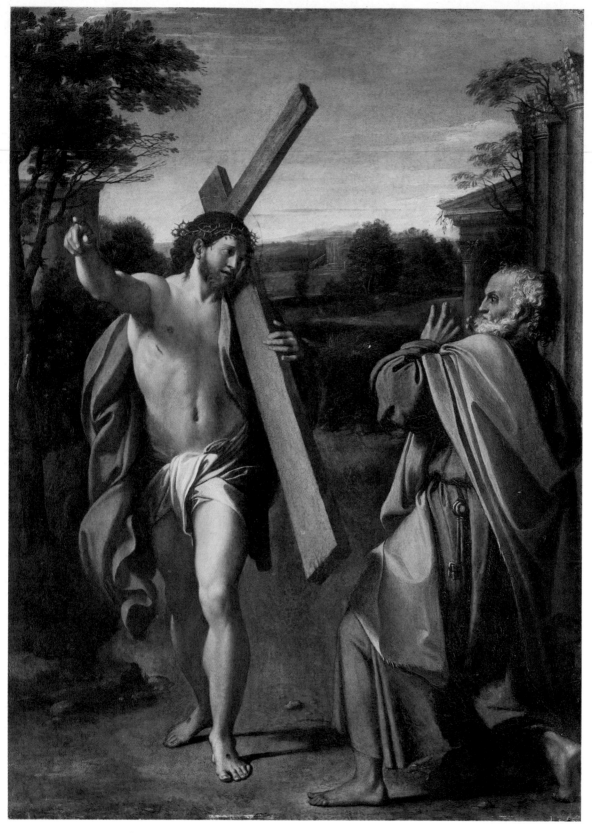

ANNIBALE CARRACCI
born Bologna 1560, died Rome 1609
Christ and St Peter on the Appian Way, 'Domine, quo vadis?' 1601/02
wood 77.4 × 56.3
Purchased 1826

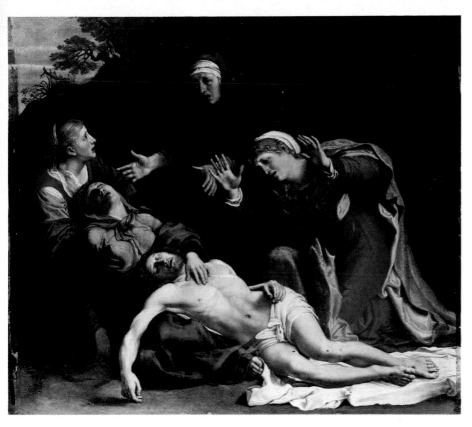

ANNIBALE CARRACCI
born Bologna 1560, died Rome 1609
*The Dead Christ Mourned, 'The
  Three Maries'* c 1604
canvas 92.8 × 103.2
Presented 1913

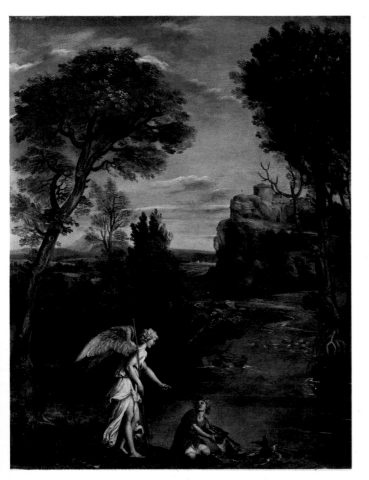

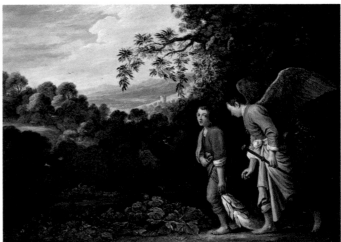

ADAM ELSHEIMER
born Frankfurt 1578, died Rome 1610
Tobias and the Archangel Raphael probably
  a late work
copper 19.3 × 27.6
Bequeathed 1894

DOMENICO ZAMPIERI called DOMENICHINO
born Bologna 1581, died Naples 1641
Landscape with Tobias and the Angel c 1617/18
copper 45.1 × 33.9
Bequeathed 1831

89

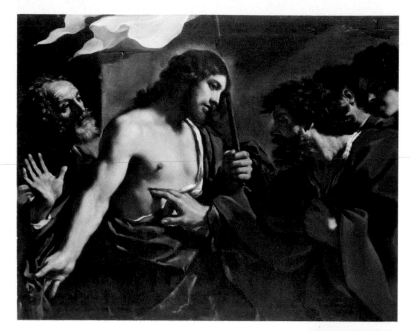

GIOVANNI FRANCESCO BARBIERI called
    GUERCINO
born Cento 1591, died Bologna 1666
The Incredulity of St Thomas 1621
canvas 115.6 × 142.5
Purchased 1917

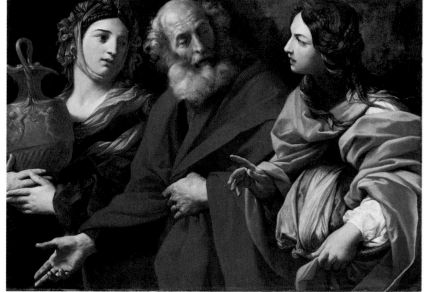

GUIDO RENI
born and died Bologna, 1575–1642
Lot and his daughters leaving Sodom c 1615/20
canvas 111.2 × 149.2
Purchased 1844

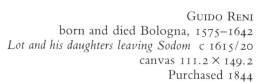

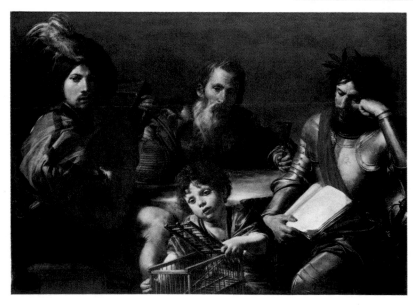

LE VALENTIN
born Coulommiers 1591(?), died Rome 1632
The Four Ages of Man
Canvas 96.5 × 134
Presented 1938

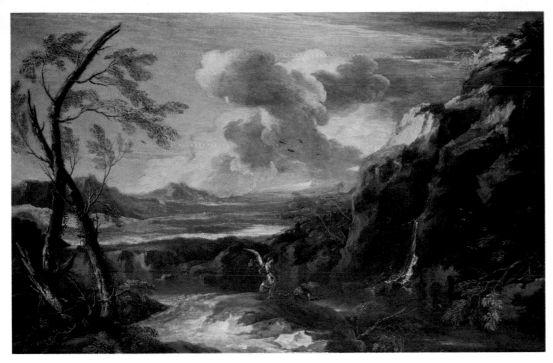

SALVATOR ROSA
born Naples 1615, died
    Rome 1673
*Landscape with Tobias and the
    Angel* a late work(?)
canvas 147.4 × 224
Purchased 1959

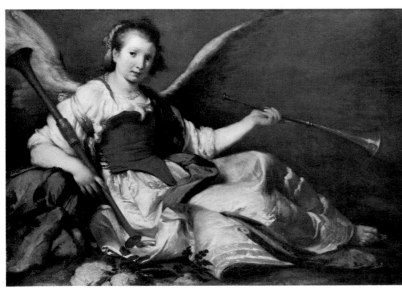

BERNARDO STROZZI
born Genoa 1581, died Venice 1644
Personification of Fame probably c 1635
canvas 106.7 × 151.7
Purchased 1961

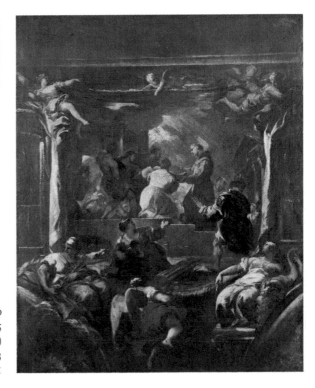

LUCA GIORDANO
born and died Naples, 1634–1705
St Anthony of Padua not later than 1700(?)
canvas 105.5 × 80.3
Presented 1901

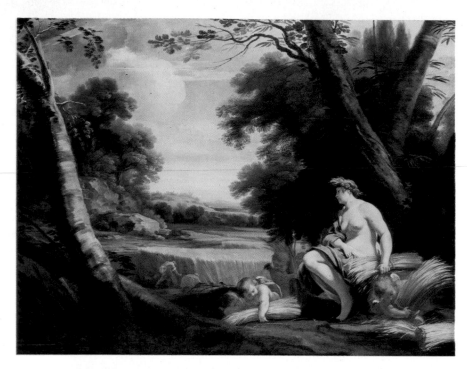

SIMON VOUET
born and died Paris, 1590–1649
Ceres and harvesting Cupids probably c 1634
canvas 147.6 × 188.7
Purchased 1958

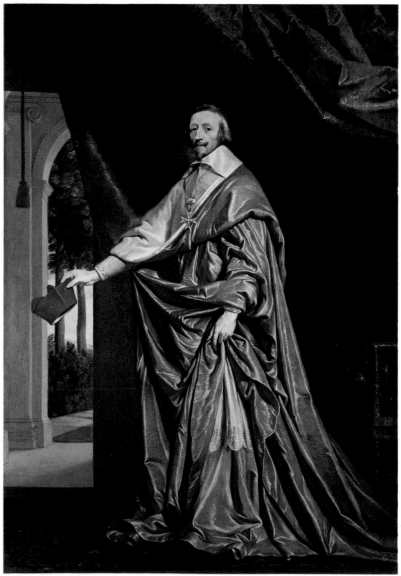

PHILIPPE DE CHAMPAIGNE
born Brussels 1602, died Paris 1674
Cardinal Richelieu c 1640(?)
canvas 259.7 × 177.8
signed
Presented 1895

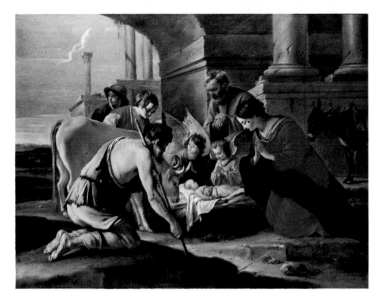

LOUIS LENAIN
born Laon c 1593, died Paris 1648
The Adoration of the Shepherds c 1640
canvas 109.5 × 137.4
Purchased 1962

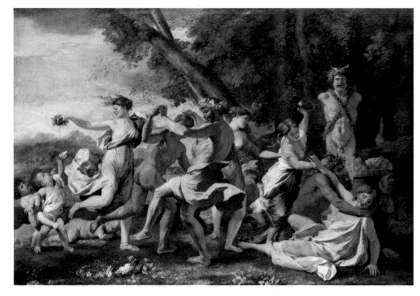

NICOLAS POUSSIN
born Les Andelys 1594, died Rome 1665
A Bacchanalian Revel probably 1630s
canvas 99.7 × 142.9
Purchased 1826

NICOLAS POUSSIN
born Les Andelys 1594, died Rome 1665
Landscape with a man killed by a snake probably 1648
canvas 119.4 × 198.8
Purchased 1947

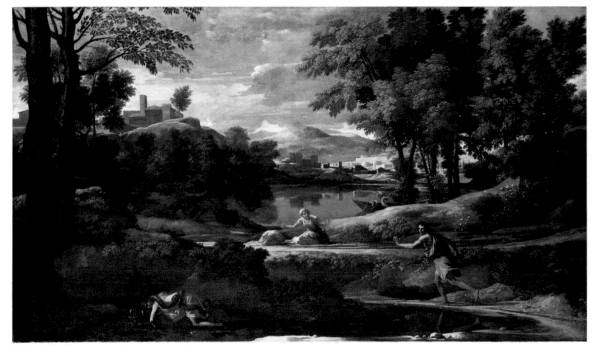

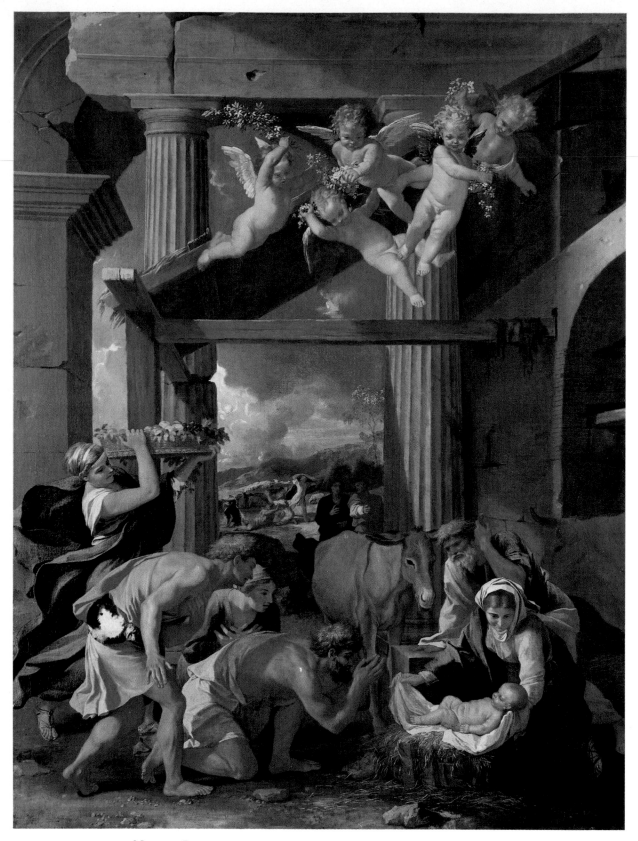

NICOLAS POUSSIN
born Les Andelys 1594, died Rome 1665
The Adoration of the Shepherds c 1637
canvas 96.5 × 73.7
signed
Purchased 1957

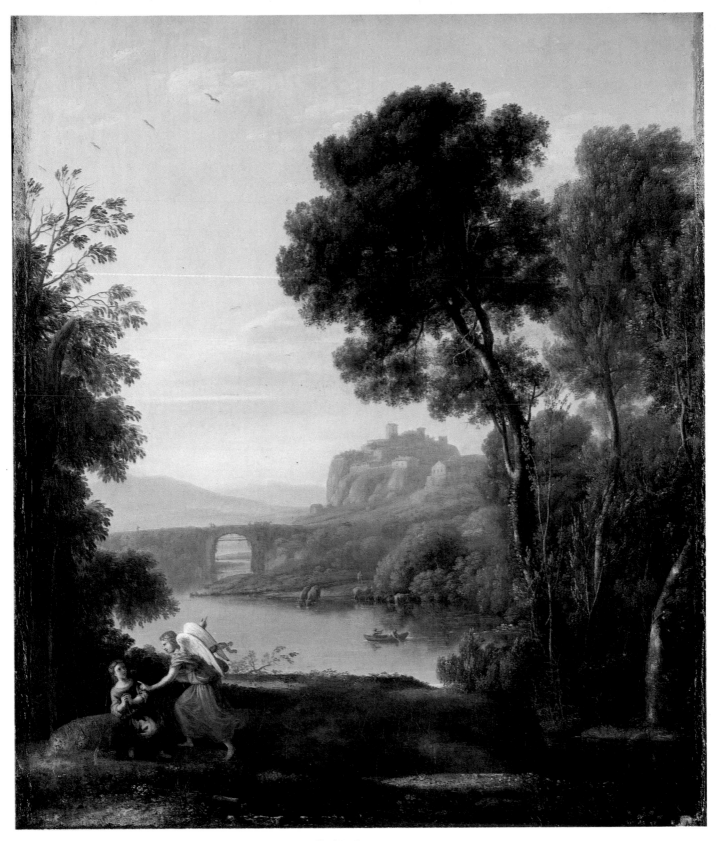

CLAUDE GELLÉE called LE LORRAIN
born Champagne 1600, died Rome 1682
Hagar and the Angel 1646
canvas, mounted on wood 52.7 × 43.8
signed and dated
Presented 1823/28

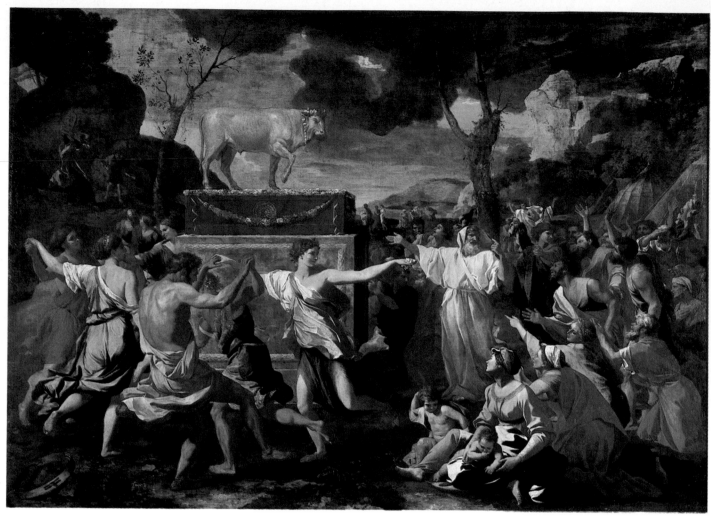

NICOLAS POUSSIN
born Les Andelys 1594, died Rome 1665
The Adoration of the Golden Calf c 1636/37
canvas on panel 154 × 214
Purchased 1945

GASPARD DUGHET
born and died Rome, 1615–1675
Ariccia an early work(?)
canvas 49 × 66.7
Bequeathed 1831

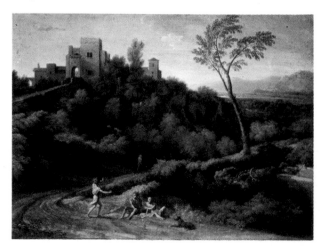

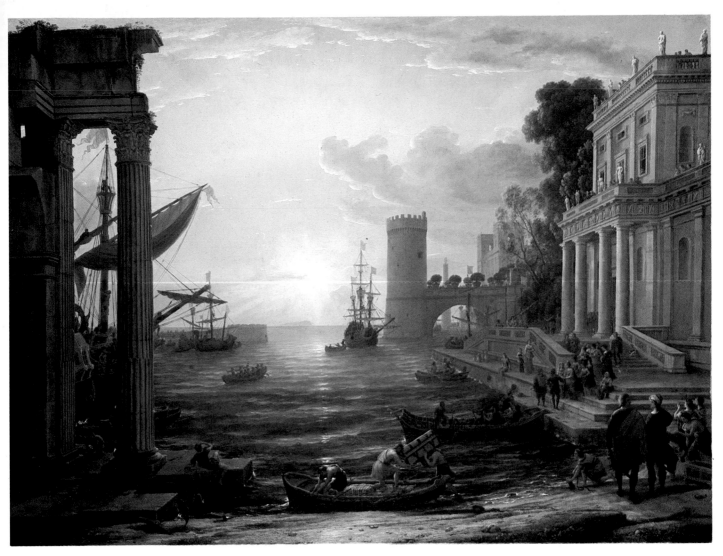

CLAUDE GELLÉE called LE LORRAIN
born Champagne 1600, died Rome 1682
The embarkation of the Queen of Sheba 1648
canvas 148.6 × 193.7
signed and dated
Purchased 1824

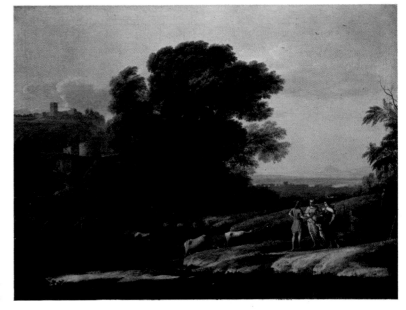

CLAUDE GELLÉE called LE LORRAIN
born Champagne 1600, died Rome 1682
Cephalus and Procris reunited by Diana 1645
canvas 101.6 × 132.1
signed and dated
Purchased 1824

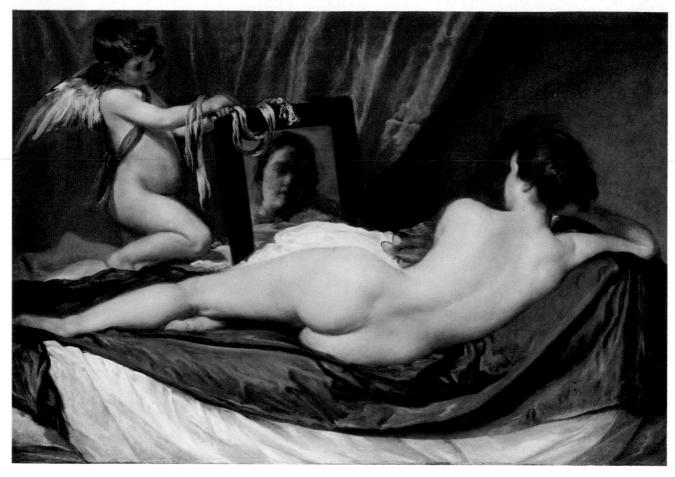

DIEGO VELÁZQUEZ
born Seville 1599, died Madrid 1660
*Kitchen scene with Christ in the house of
   Martha and Mary* 1618
canvas 60 × 103.5
dated
Bequeathed 1892

DIEGO VELÁZQUEZ
born Seville 1599, died Madrid 1660
The Toilet of Venus, 'The Rokeby Venus'
   probably c 1648/49
canvas 122.5 × 177
Presented 1906

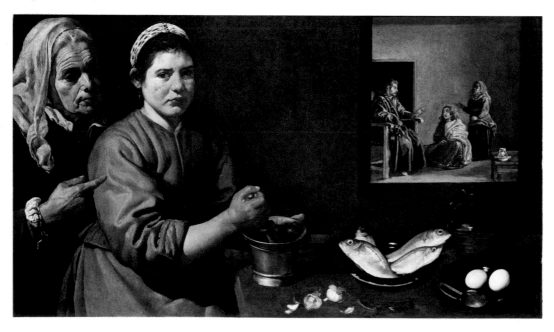

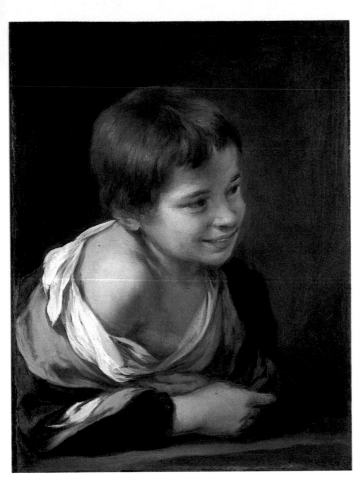

BARTOLOMÉ ESTEBAN MURILLO
born and died Seville, 1617–1682
A peasant boy leaning on a sill a late work
canvas 52 × 38.5
Presented 1826

BARTOLOMÉ ESTEBAN MURILLO
born and died Seville, 1617–1682
Self-portrait c 1670/5
canvas 122 × 107
Inscribed on tablet: 'Murillo portraying himself to
fulfil the wishes and prayers of his children'
Purchased 1953

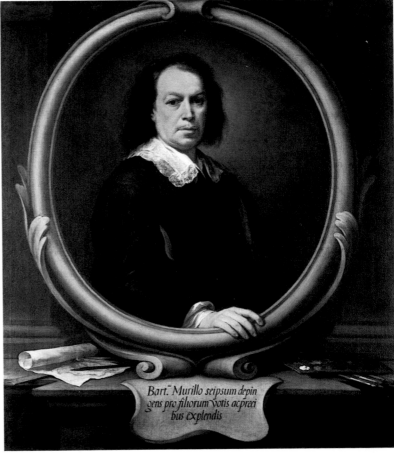

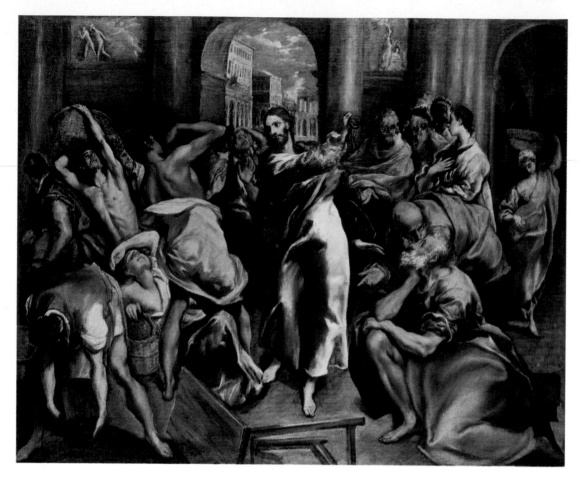

DOMENIKOS THEOTOKOPOULOS called EL GRECO
born Candia 1541, died Toledo 1614
Christ driving the traders from the Temple
    probably c 1600
canvas 106.3 × 129.7
Presented 1895

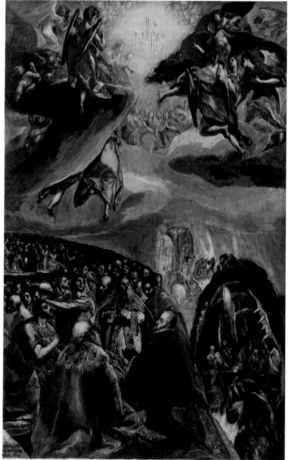

DOMENIKOS THEOTOKOPOULOS called EL GRECO
born Candia 1541, died Toledo 1614
The Adoration of the Name of Jesus
probably c 1580
wood 57.8 × 34.2
signed
Purchased 1955

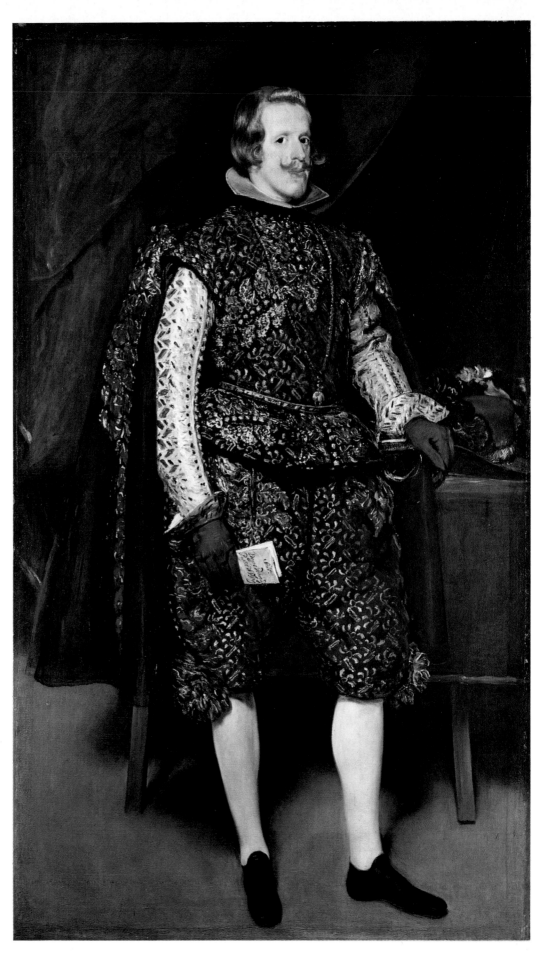

DIEGO VELÁZQUEZ
born Seville 1599, died Madrid
1660
*Philip IV of Spain in brown and
silver* c 1631
canvas 195 × 110
signed
Purchased 1882

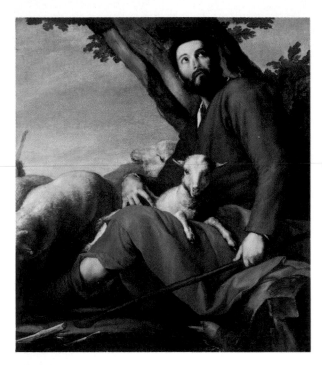

JUSEPE DE RIBERA
born Játiva 1591(?), died Naples 1652
Jacob with the flock of Laban (fragment) 1638
canvas 132 × 118
signed and dated
Bequeathed 1854

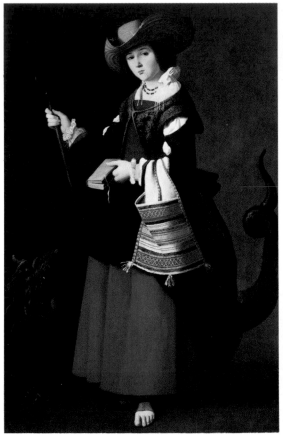

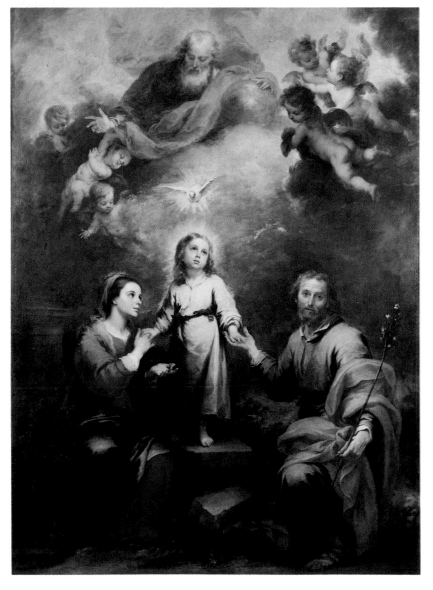

FRANCISCO DE ZURBARAN
born Fuente de Cantos 1598, died
    Madrid 1664
St Margaret probably early 1630s
canvas 163 × 105
Purchased 1903

BARTOLOMÉ ESTEBAN MURILLO
born and died Seville, 1617–1682
The Two Trinities, 'The Pedroso Murillo' c 1681/82
canvas 293 × 207
Purchased 1837

The eighteenth century

With the exception of British painters, particularly the portraitists who were directly employed by the aristocracy, and Canaletto, whose work was more popular with English buyers than with Italians, European artists of the eighteenth century have never been much favoured by English collectors. Consequently, the eighteenth century is still thinly represented at the National Gallery despite recent purchases in this field.

During the Gallery's early years the only pictures of the previous century to enter the collection were Hogarth's series '*Marriage à la Mode*' and Reynold's *Lord Heathfield*, all purchased in 1824 with the Angerstein pictures, Gainsborough's *Watering place* (p 117), presented in 1827, two landscapes by Richard Wilson, part of the Beaumont gift, and one foreign picture, the famous '*Stonemason's yard*' by Canaletto (p 117), which had also been in the Angerstein collection. Not until 1836, when four small pictures by Lancret representing *The Ages of Man* were accepted as part of the bequest of Lt Col Ollney, did the Gallery possess any example of French eighteenth-century painting, and acquisitions continued to be made with great infrequency, in most cases by gift or bequest.

Canaletto had been much admired in the eighteenth century for the detailed naturalism and accuracy of his views, which appealed to English collectors more than the playful and essentially untruthful illusionism of other Venetian painters. Many English visitors returned from Italy with examples of his work, and during his visits to England in the 1740s and 50s he was much sought after to paint views of English country houses. So while many examples of his work were bequeathed to the Gallery in the nineteenth century, his contemporary, and probably the greatest Venetian painter of the eighteenth century, Giambattista Tiepolo, remained poorly represented. The ceiling painting showing *An allegory with Venus and Time* (p 106), the only large-scale example of his decorative work in the Gallery, was purchased at auction in 1969 shortly after its discovery in the Egyptian Embassy in London.

No effort was made in the nineteenth century to acquire French pictures because the Rococo, which had always been looked on with suspicion by the English, continued to be regarded as both frivolous and immoral. Although Hogarth, who visited Paris on more than one occasion, was indebted to French art for his delicate and fluid brushwork, he combined this with a strong satirical and moralising vein which distinguishes his work from the voluptuous mythologies of Boucher (p 114) and the charming domestic scenes of Lancret (p 114). At times Hogarth's satire is even directed specifically against the French, against their libertinism and religious superstition. In the nineteenth century, as a concern for morality grew stronger in England, so also did these prejudices, which were reinforced by patriotic feeling.

Nevertheless French Rococo did leave its imprint on English painting, particularly on the 'conversation piece' where groups are commonly shown in pastoral settings. French engravers, such as Philippe Mercier and Gravelot, a pupil of Boucher, were responsible for disseminating in England through their prints a type of composition which derives from the *fête galantes* of Jean-Antoine Watteau. Gainsborough was certainly familiar with their work, and although *Mr and Mrs Andrews* (p 120) are depicted in contemporary dress with the well-regulated fields of their own estate spreading out behind, the type of composition and the elegant figures have their origin in such pictures as Watteau's '*La Gamme d'Amour*' (p 110) where the setting is undefined and the figures masquerade in fancy costume. Gainsborough probably approaches closest to the French in his very late portraits such as *The morning walk* (p 118). Hardness and precise definition give way to an atmospheric evocation of place and mood, conveyed by loose feathery brushwork and silvery tones.

Fortunately, the French eighteenth-century collection has lately been enriched by a number of important acquisitions. In 1972 what may be Lancret's masterpiece, '*La Tasse du Chocolat*' (p 114), was bequeathed to the Gallery. With its fanciful treatment of nature it makes an interesting contrast to the straightforward realism of Gainsborough's contemporaneous portrait of *Mr and Mrs Andrews*. An imposing portrait of the financier *Antoine Paris* (p 109) by Hyacinthe Rigaud, one of the foremost portraitists of the early eighteenth century, was purchased in 1975, and in 1976 so was a portrait by Perronneau of *Jacques Cazotte* (p 115), which in its intimacy and spiritedness is entirely characteristic of its era.

However, the two recent acquisitions in this field of greatest importance have both coincidentally come to the Gallery from the Rosebery collection at Mentmore. Drouais' full-length portrait of *Madame de Pompadour* (p 112), completed after her death in 1764, was purchased in 1977 by private treaty sale, and shows Louis xv's mistress gorgeously arrayed in a dress of flowered silk in her rooms at Versailles working at a tapestry frame. The other picture was sold at the Mentmore sale in 1977 as a *Toilet of Venus* by Carle Van Loo, and was afterwards discovered by its buyer, David Carritt, to be an important early work of Fragonard, executed in 1753 while he was a student at the École des Élèves Protégés, depicting *Psyche showing her sisters her gifts from Cupid* (p 111). It was subsequently purchased by the Gallery, and besides being the sole work by Fragonard, is also the only work of its type and period in the Collection.

The majority of the British pictures are today exhibited at the Tate Gallery, but among the small selection that remains at Trafalgar Square are works of the highest quality. Reynolds can be seen both in the heroic mood of *General Sir Banastre Tarleton* (p 119) and in the more intimate vein of *Anne, Countess of Albemarle* (p 120). The Gallery also possesses a striking and accomplished portrait by Sir Thomas Lawrence of *Queen Charlotte*, the wife of George iii (p 121). Lawrence, who later became President of the Royal Academy, was only twenty when he painted this picture in 1789. A different type of English portraiture, more purely classical than that of Reynolds, Gainsborough or Lawrence, is exemplified by George Stubbs' *Milbanke and Melbourne families* (p 116), which was purchased in 1975. In this group portrait he avoids all rhetoric, and succeeds solely by the careful positioning of each detail and the balancing of the tones in conferring upon his sitters a calm and unassailable dignity.

At the end of the eighteenth century and beginning of the nineteenth century one of the greatest artists of the period, Francisco de Goya, was working at the Spanish Court in what had become an artistic backwater. Yet during his long life he witnessed the upheaval of Europe, and succeeded in chronicling the very great changes of thought and feeling that accompanied it. The small witchcraft scene (p 122), which was purchased in 1896, is no longer eighteenth century in feeling but seems to question man's ability to govern himself by reason. The subject is here drawn from a Spanish play, and, as in many of Goya's etchings, the real world is replaced by an imaginary one, peopled by frightening apparitions. *The Duke of Wellington* (p 122), purchased in 1961, is the last of his works to enter the collection. It was painted during Wellington's first visit to Madrid in 1812, when the British army liberated the city from the French, but some of the decorations were added subsequently.

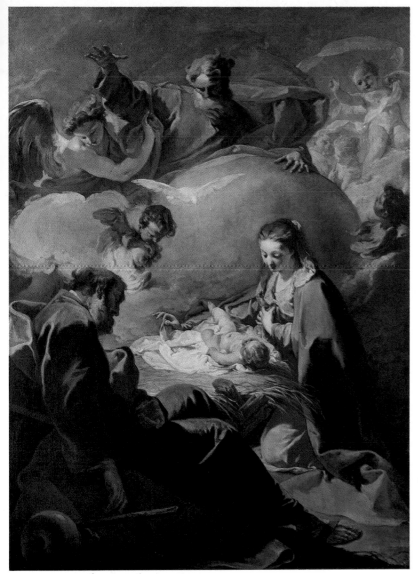

GIOVANNI BATTISTA PITTONI
born and died Venice, 1687–1767
The Nativity with God the Father and the Holy Ghost
   c 1740
canvas 222.7 × 153.5
Purchased 1958

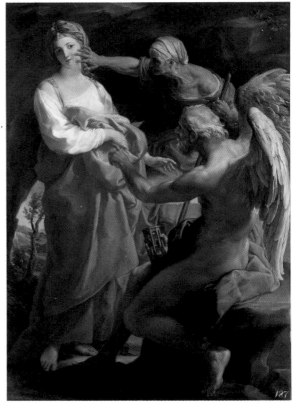

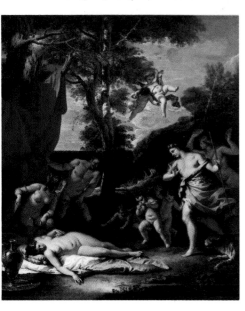

SEBASTIANO RICCI
born Belluno 1659,
   died Venice 1734
Bacchus and Ariadne
   c 1710(?)
canvas 75.9 × 63.2
Purchased 1871

POMPEO GIROLAMO BATONI
born Lucca 1708, died Rome 1787
Time orders Old Age to destroy Beauty   1746
canvas 135.3 × 96.5
signed and dated
Purchased 1961

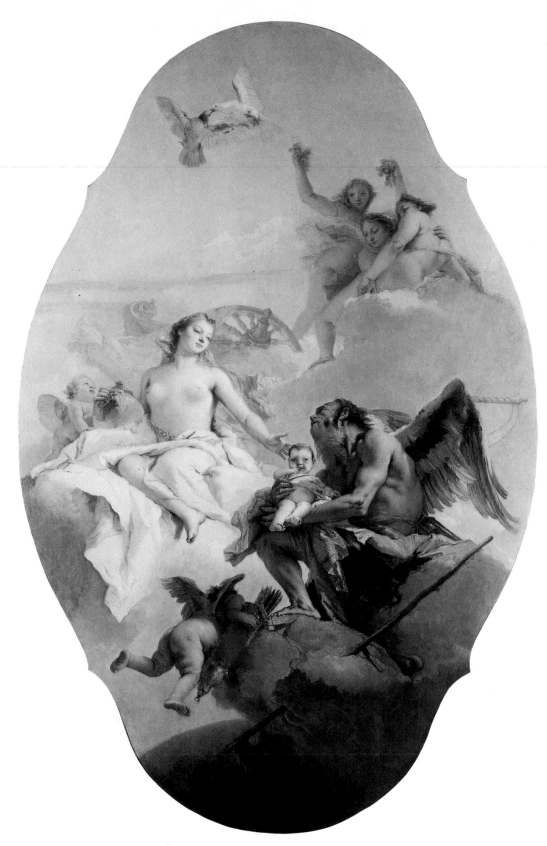

GIOVANNI BATTISTA TIEPOLO
born Venice 1696, died Madrid 1770
An allegory with Venus and Time c 1754
canvas 292.1 × 190.4
Purchased 1969

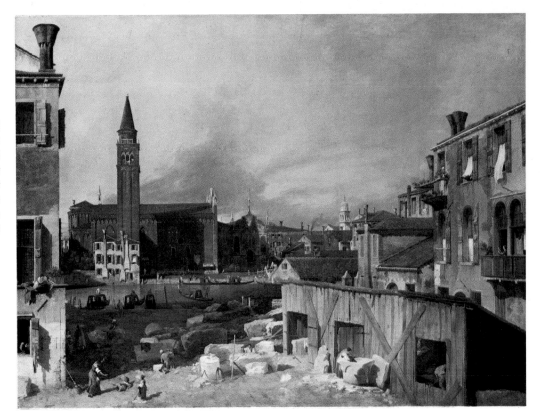

GIOVANNI ANTONIO CANAL called
CANALETTO
born and died Venice, 1697–1768
Venice: Campo St Vidal and St
Maria della Carità, 'The
stonemason's yard' c 1730
canvas 123.8 × 162.9
Presented 1823/28

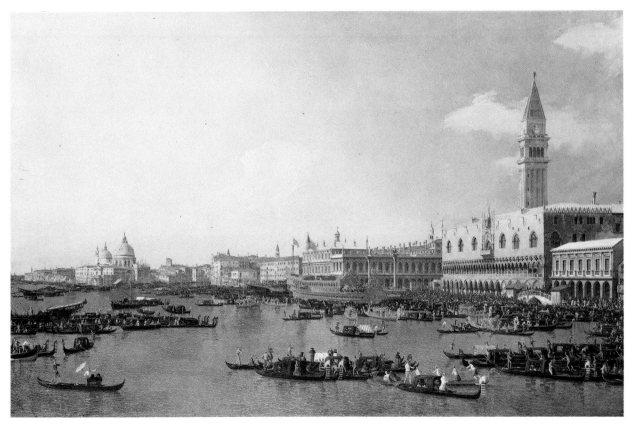

GIOVANNI ANTONIO CANAL called CANALETTO
born and died Venice, 1697–1768
Venice: The basin of S. Marco on Ascension Day c 1735/41(?)
canvas 121.9 × 182.9
Bequeathed 1929

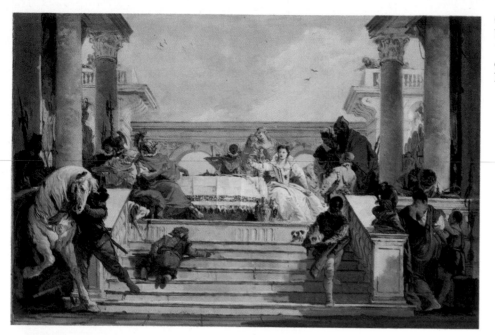

GIOVANNI BATTISTA TIEPOLO
born Venice 1696, died Madrid 1770
The banquet of Cleopatra c 1745
canvas 44.2 × 65.7
Purchased 1972

GIOVANNI DOMENICO TIEPOLO
born and died Venice, 1727–1804
*The procession of the Trojan Horse into
Troy* (one of a series)
canvas 38.8 × 66.7
Purchased 1918

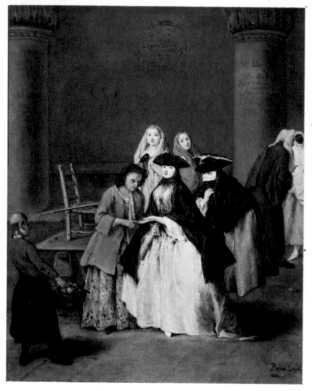

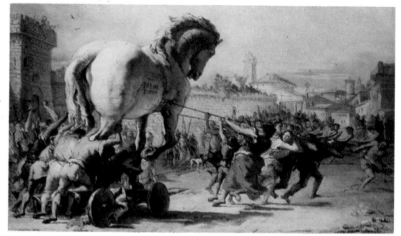

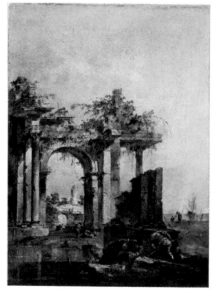

PIETRO LONGHI
born and died Venice, 1702(?)–1785
A fortune-teller at Venice 1756
canvas 59.1 × 48.6
signed and dated
Purchased 1891

FRANCESCO GUARDI
born and died Venice, 1712–1793
A caprice with ruins on the seashore
probably mid 1770s
canvas 36.8 × 26.1
Bequeathed 1910

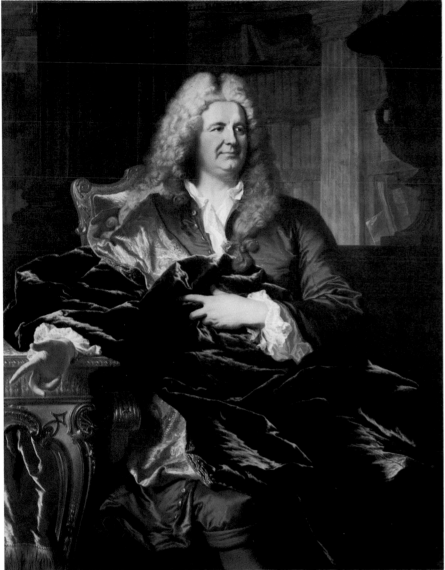

HYACINTHE RIGAUD
born Perpignan 1659, died Paris 1743
Portrait of Antoine Paris 1724
canvas 144.7 × 110.5
Purchased 1975

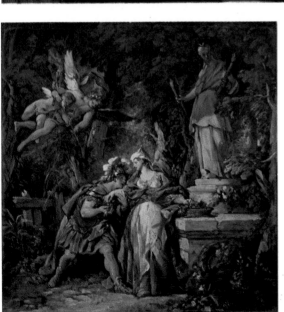

JEAN-MARC NATTIER
born and died Paris, 1685–1766
Manon Balletti 1757
canvas 54 × 45.7
signed and dated
Bequeathed 1945

JEAN-FRANÇOIS DETROY
born Paris 1679, died Rome 1752
Jason swearing eternal affection to Medea c 1743
canvas 56.5 × 52.1
Bequeathed 1962

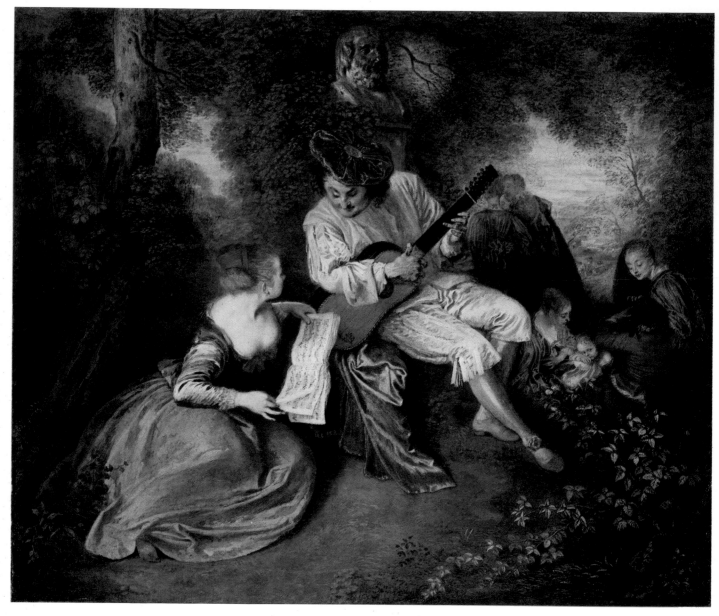

JEAN-ANTOINE WATTEAU
born Valenciennes 1684, died Nogent 1721
'La Gamme d'Amour' probably a late work
canvas 50.8 × 59.7
Bequeathed 1912

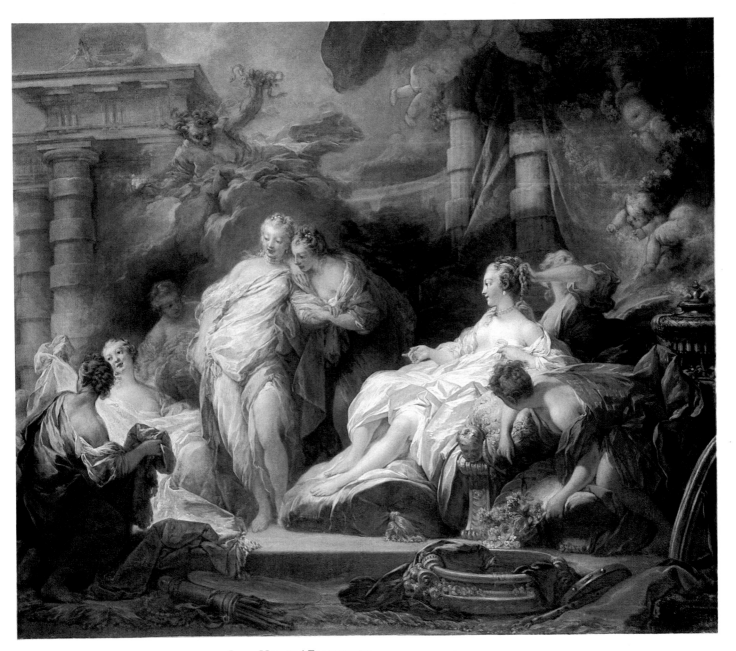

JEAN-HONORÉ FRAGONARD
born Grasse 1732, died Paris 1806
Psyche showing her sisters her gifts from Cupid 1753
canvas 168 × 192
Purchased 1978

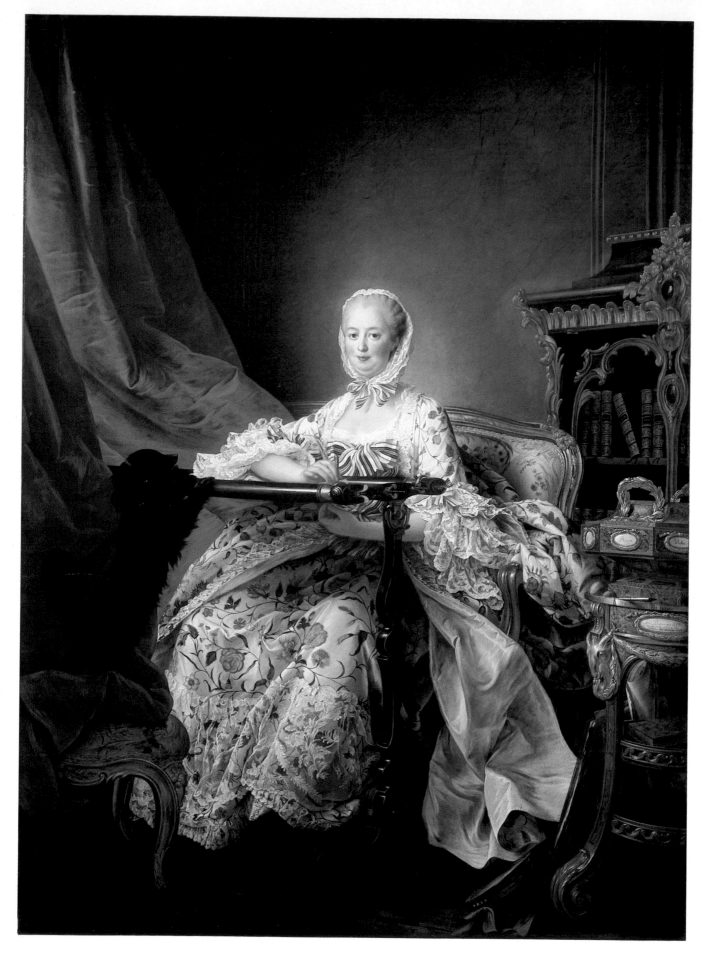

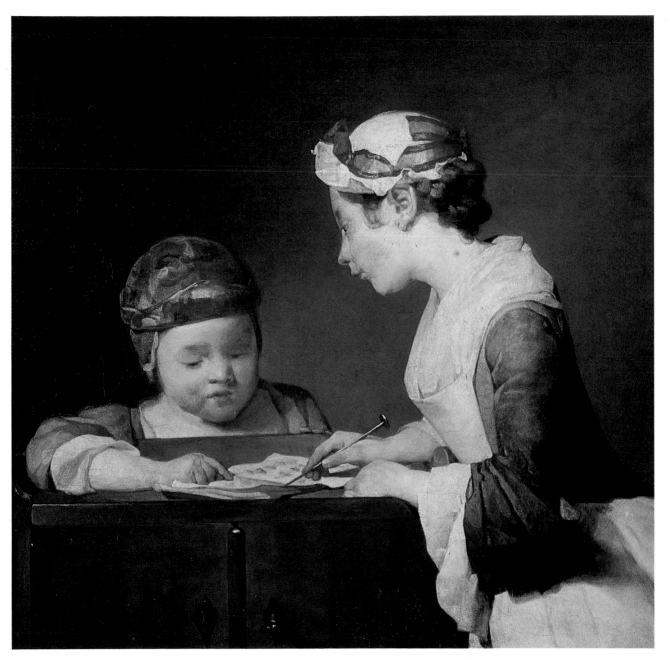

JEAN-SIMÉON CHARDIN
born and died Paris, 1699–1779
The young schoolmistress 1740(?)
canvas 61.6 × 66.7
Bequeathed 1925

FRANÇOIS-HUBERT DROUAIS
born and died Paris, 1727–1775
Madame de Pompadour 1763/64
canvas 217 × 157
signed and dated
Purchased 1977

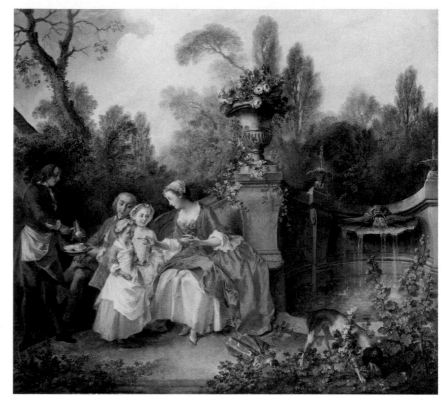

NICOLAS LANCRET
born and died Paris, 1690–1743
A lady and gentleman with two girls in a
garden, 'La Tasse de Chocolat' 1742
canvas 88.9 × 97.8
Bequeathed 1973

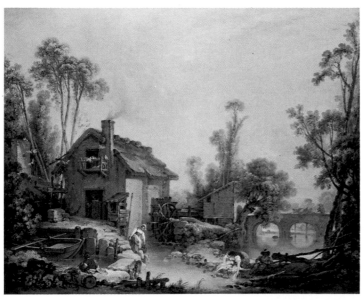

FRANÇOIS BOUCHER
born and died Paris, 1703–1770
Landscape with a watermill 1755
canvas 57.2 × 73
sgned and dated
Purchased 1966

FRANÇOIS BOUCHER
born and died Paris, 1703–1770
Pan and Syrinx 1759
canvas 32.4 × 41.9
signed and dated
Presented 1880

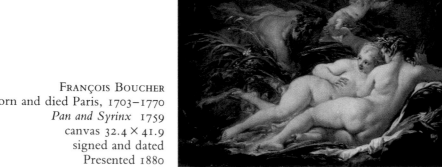

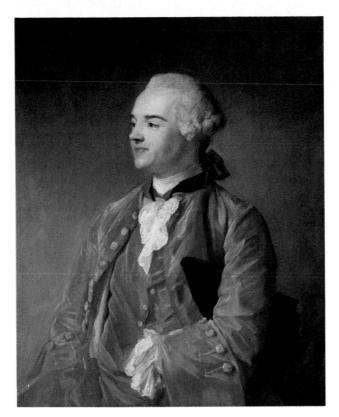

JEAN-BAPTISTE PERRONNEAU
born Paris 1715(?), died Amsterdam 1783
Portrait of Jacques Cazotte
canvas 89.5 × 71.9
Purchased 1976

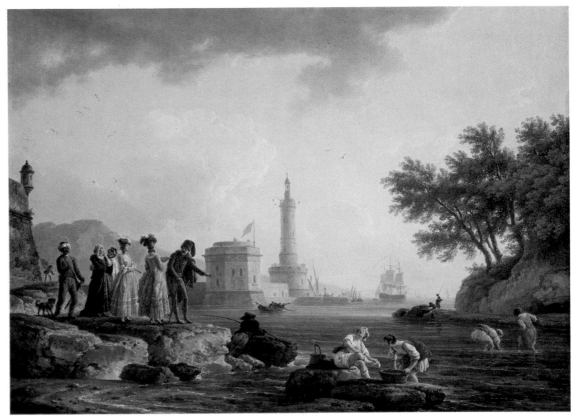

CLAUDE-JOSEPH VERNET
born Avignon 1714, died Paris 1789
A sea-shore 1776
copper 62.2 × 85.1
signed and dated
Bequeathed 1846/47

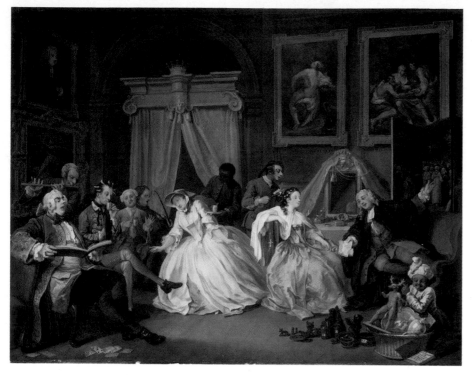

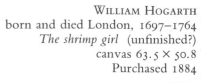

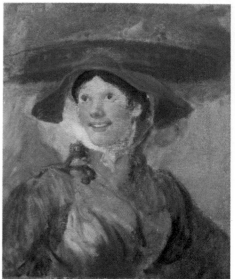

WILLIAM HOGARTH
born and died London, 1697–1764
The shrimp girl (unfinished?)
canvas 63.5 × 50.8
Purchased 1884

WILLIAM HOGARTH
born and died London, 1697–1764
The countess's morning levée (one of a series called '*Marriage à la Mode*') 1743
canvas 70.5 × 90.8
Purchased 1824

GEORGE STUBBS
born Liverpool 1724, died London 1806
The Milbanke and Melbourne Families c 1770
canvas 97.2 × 149.3
Purchased 1975

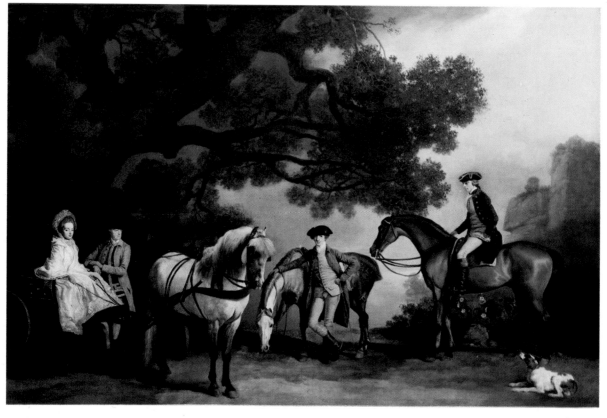

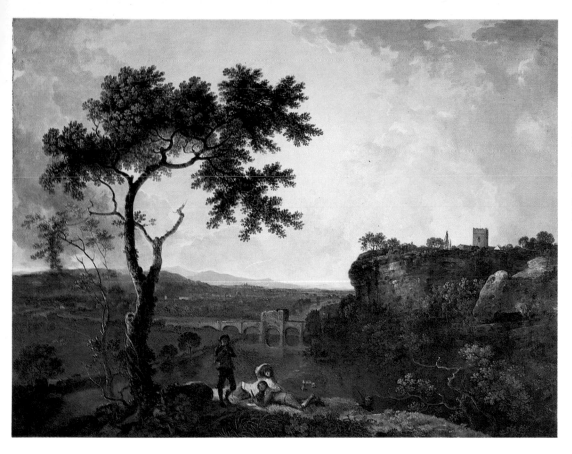

RICHARD WILSON
born Penegoes 1713/14,
    died Colmmendy 1782
Holt Bridge on the River Dee
    1762
canvas 148.5 × 193
Purchased 1953

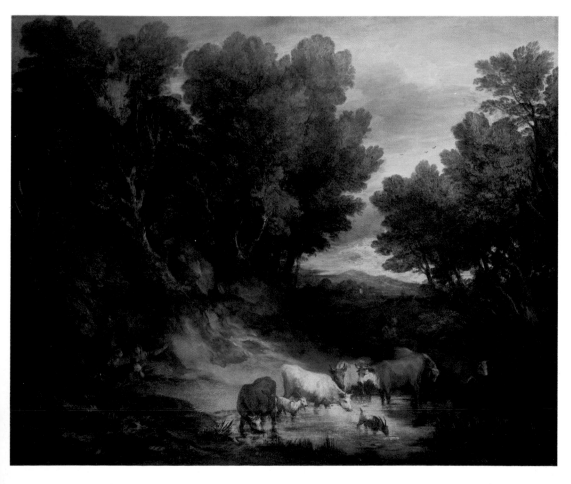

THOMAS GAINSBOROUGH
born Sudbury 1728, died
    London 1788
The watering place 1777
canvas 147.3 × 180.3
Presented 1827

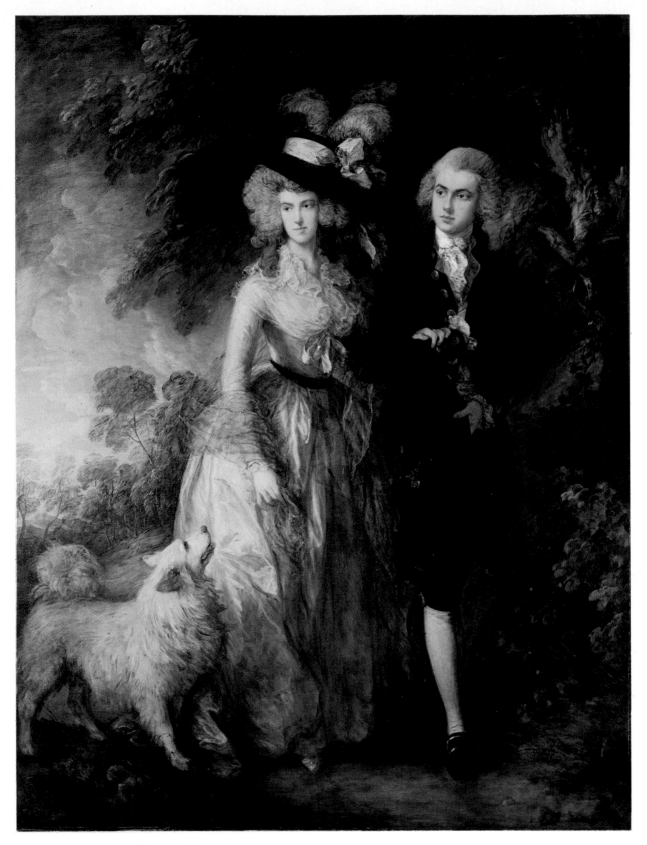

THOMAS GAINSBOROUGH
born Sudbury 1728, died London 1788
The morning walk 1785/86
canvas 236.3 × 179.1
Purchased 1954

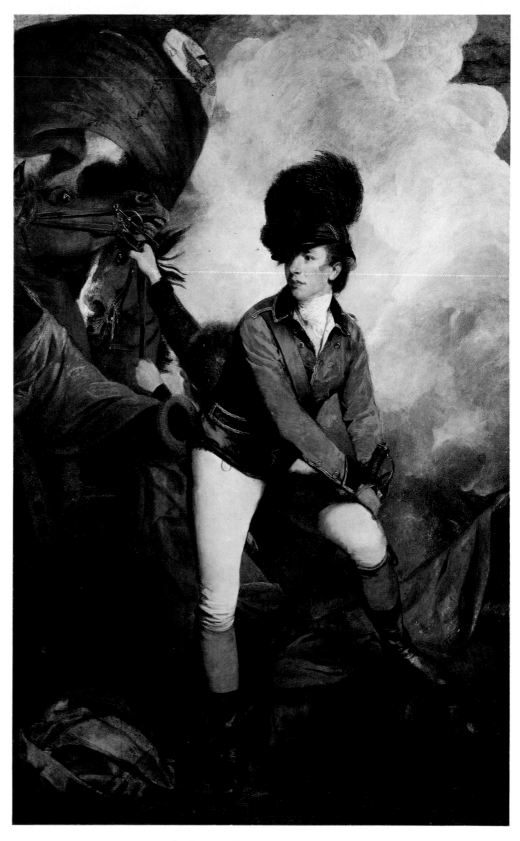

Sir Joshua Reynolds
born Plympton 1723, died London 1792
General Sir Banastre Tarleton 1782
canvas 236.2 × 145.4
Bequeathed 1951

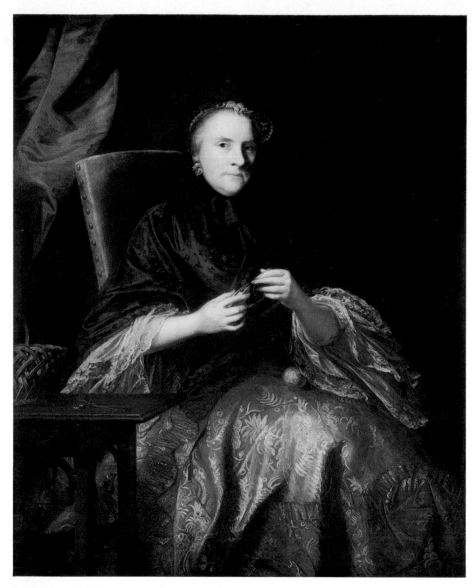

SIR JOSHUA REYNOLDS
born Plympton 1723, died London 1792
Anne, Countess of Albemarle 1757(?)
canvas 126.4 × 101
Purchased 1888/90

THOMAS GAINSBOROUGH
born Sudbury 1728, died London
  1788
Mr and Mrs Andrews c 1750
canvas 69.8 × 119.4
Purchased 1960

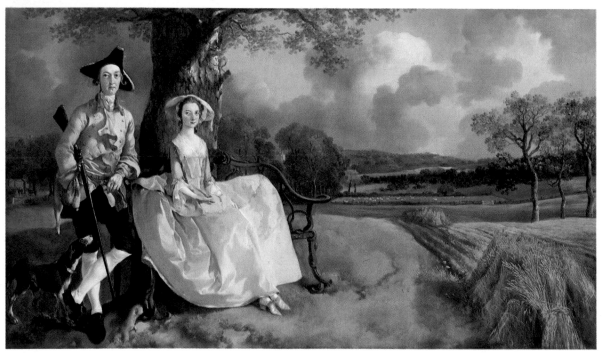

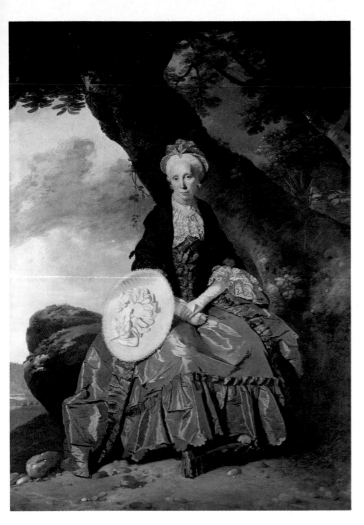

JOHANN ZOFFANY
born Frankfurt on the Main 1733(?),
    died Strand-on-the-Green 1810
Mrs Oswald 1760(?)
canvas 226.5 × 158.8
Purchased 1938

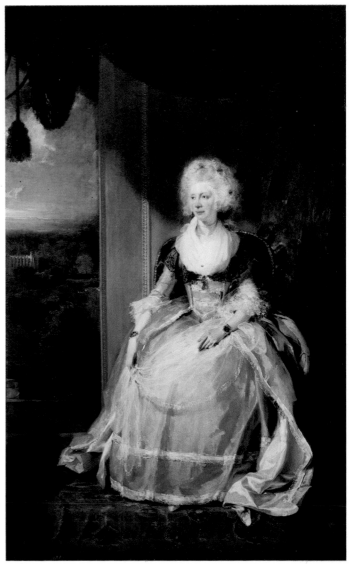

SIR THOMAS LAWRENCE
born Bristol 1769, died London 1830
Queen Charlotte 1789
canvas 239.4 × 147.3
Purchased 1927

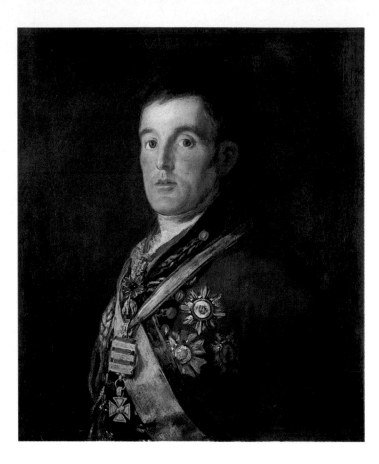

FRANCISCO DE GOYA
born Fuendetodos 1746, died Bordeaux 1828
The Duke of Wellington 1812/14
wood 64.3 × 52.4
Purchased 1961

FRANCISCO DE GOYA
born Fuendetodos 1746, died Bordeaux 1828
Doña Isabel de Porcel 1805
canvas 82 × 54.6
Purchased 1896

FRANCISCO DE GOYA
born Fuendetodos 1746, died Bordeaux
1828
A scene from 'The Forcibly Bewitched'
canvas 42.5 × 30.8
Purchased 1896

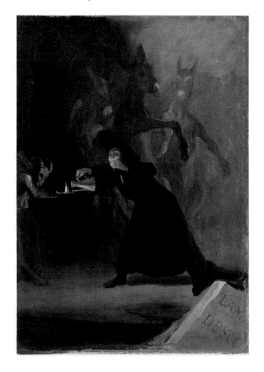

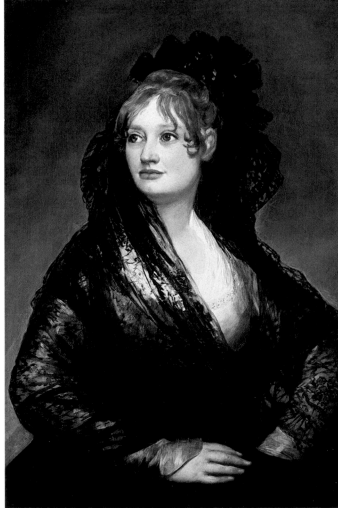

The nineteenth century and after

Despite increased efforts in recent years to make up the deficiency, the nineteenth century is one of the most poorly represented periods in the Gallery. There is still, for instance, no example of the work of Jacques-Louis David or the German Romantics, and such major painters of the first half of the century as Delacroix and Ingres are represented by only a handful of works. Yet at the time of the Gallery's foundation it was never suggested that the collection should exclude the work of contemporary artists. These deficiencies can fairly be attributed to the acquisition policy of those nineteenth-century directors, Eastlake, Boxall and Burton, who so enriched the Gallery's collection with Italian painting. By 1900, in fact, no painting by a foreign artist of the nineteenth century had been purchased, and the seven foreign works of this period that had been acquired as gifts or bequests were by artists who today are virtually forgotten.

Even the British collection had been formed without any considerable financial commitment. In 1847 the Vernon gift had contributed about 400 pictures, almost all British, and they were followed in 1856 by the Turner bequest of over 280 paintings and almost 2000 drawings and watercolours. Owing to the shortage of space at Trafalgar Square, Vernon's pictures were first shown at his own house and later at Marlborough House, where they were joined by the Turners. So from the beginning these modern works were segregated from the old masters which formed the core of the collection. In 1859 they moved to the new South Kensington Museum (now known as the Victoria and Albert Museum) and finally in 1897 to the Tate. Today only a small selection remains at Trafalgar Square, including Constable's *Cornfield*, which was donated in 1837 by a group of the artist's admirers after his death, and such celebrated Turners as *The Fighting Téméraire* (p 125) and *Rain, steam and speed* (p 126). Two more of his works, *Dido building Carthage* and a harbour scene in which he emulates traditional modes of landscape, hang with the seventeenth-century French pictures between works by Claude, in accordance with Turner's wishes.

Neither Eastlake nor his successors seem to have had much sympathy or admiration for the modern continental schools of painting. 'A crying defect', Eastlake wrote, 'in all French painters, though perhaps not so much their fault as their country's, is that *goût libre* which is such a terrible abuse of the art and which our countrymen are happily free from, with one or two exceptions'. At the end of the century the Impressionists met with even greater contempt.

The French paintings which entered the Gallery as part of the Salting bequest in 1910 were not at that time either modern or avant-garde. Although he had chosen Dutch and Italian pictures with such discrimination, Salting's taste in nineteenth century works was conservative. Of these the majority were of the Barbizon School, including paintings by T. Rousseau and Daubigny and seven by Corot. Also among the Salting pictures were two very fine oil sketches by Constable, a famous view of Weymouth bay and *Salisbury Cathedral* (p 126).

Sir Hugh Lane's collection, which came to the Gallery on his death in 1917, was far more progressive in character, including a number of major Impressionist works. Although small in scale, Manet's *Music in the Tuileries Gardens* (p 133) of 1862 shows the artist depicting contemporary life in a forthright style which successfully avoids the sterile formulae of nineteenth century academic painting. In *The umbrellas* (p 135), an important picture of twenty years later, Renoir shows a similar scene, but can be observed moving away from the blurred forms of his earlier works towards a more linear and structured art. Pissarro's *View from Louveciennes* (p 134) is a masterpiece of early Impressionism, and another of the Lane pictures, *Avignon from the west* (p 127), is the finest Corot in the Gallery. Here, as a result of concentrated observation, Corot succeeds by the simplest of means in assimilating all the varied forms of the landscape into a structural and tonal harmony.

So unenthusiastic was the Trustees' response to Sir Hugh Lane's proposal to leave his collection to the Gallery that shortly before his death he changed his will and in an unwitnessed codicil left the pictures to the city of Dublin. Consequently, although legally the pictures belong to London, they are at present divided between the two cities. However, only a year after the Lane Bequest in 1918 the Gallery showed great forethought and acquired a number of important works at the sale of the collection of Edgar Degas, who had died in 1917. They included the surviving fragments of one of Manet's versions of *The execution of the Emperor Maximilian*, no less than four Ingres, a flowerpiece by Gauguin, Delacroix's early portrait of *Baron Schwiter* (p 128) and a number of drawings now at the British Museum.

Many of the Gallery's Impressionist pictures have been acquired through the generosity of another benefactor, Samuel Courtauld, who in 1923, in an effort 'to gain recognition of this School among the English public', gave £50,000 to set up a fund for the purchase of examples for the nation. Altogether just over twenty works were bought, including Monet's *Beach at Trouville* (p 134), Manet's *The Waitress* (p 133), Seurat's *Bathers, Asnières* (p 136) (possibly the masterpiece of this short-lived artist) four paintings by Degas and all four of the Gallery's works by Vincent van Gogh.

In recompense for past neglect and in recognition of the master status of the great painters of the nineteenth century, the Gallery has concentrated much of its resources in recent years on expanding this part of the collection. A number of works recently acquired are by artists not previously represented whose work is especially rare in England: 'Le Douanier' Rousseau (p 140), Gustave Moreau, Odilon Redon (p 141) and Gustav Klimt (p 141). Their paintings show the direction in which many artists moved in reaction to the naturalistic aesthetic of the Realist and Impressionist movements. Some of the gaps in the earlier part of the period have also been filled. A characteristic late religious picture by Delacroix (p 130) was purchased in 1976, and in 1978 Millet's *The winnower* (p 131), a work of major importance executed at the time of the 1848 Revolution and long believed destroyed, was bought at auction in New York.

Especially exciting among these recent acquisitions are two twentieth-century paintings, the *Portrait of Greta Moll* (p 142) of 1908 by Henri Matisse and a Cubist work of 1914 by Pablo Picasso, *Bowl of fruit, bottle and violin* (p 142). They are the first works by these artists to enter the Gallery's Collection, although the Tate Gallery at Millbank, the National Collection of Modern Painting, holds examples of them both. It is nevertheless proper that as Matisse and Picasso and other painters achieve classic status and cease to be truly 'modern' to become timeless, prime examples of their work should be acquired by the National Gallery, where they can be seen in a European context encompassing the best of all periods, back to Duccio in fourteenth-century Siena and Van Eyck in fifteenth-century Bruges.

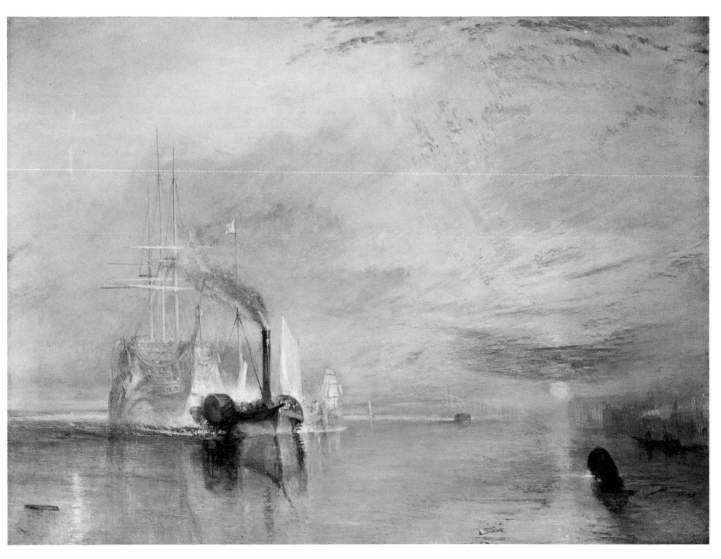

JOSEPH MALLORD WILLIAM TURNER
born and died London, 1775–1851
The 'Fighting Téméraire' 1838
canvas 90.8 × 121.9
Bequeathed 1856

JOSEPH MALLORD WILLIAM TURNER
born and died London, 1775–1851
*Rain, steam and speed – the Great
Western Railway* 1844
canvas 90.8 × 121.9
Bequeathed 1856

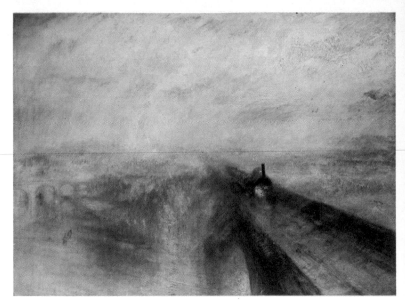

JOHN CONSTABLE
born and died East Bergholt, 1776–1837
The Haywain 1821
canvas 130.2 × 185.4
signed and dated
Presented 1886

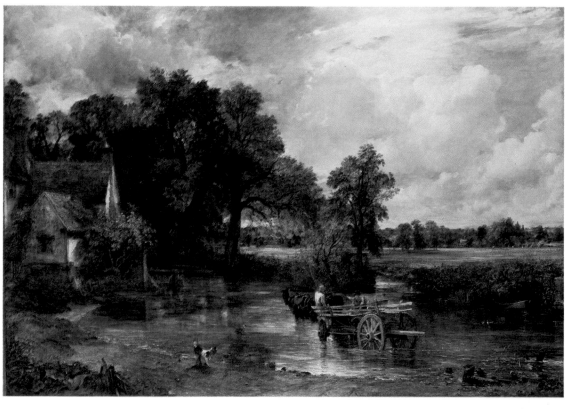

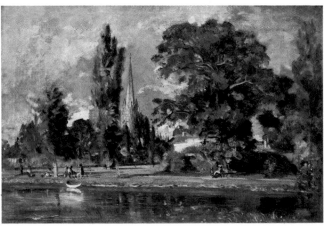

JOHN CONSTABLE
born and died East Bergholt, 1776–1837
Salisbury Cathedral c 1820
canvas 52.7 × 76.8
Bequeathed 1910

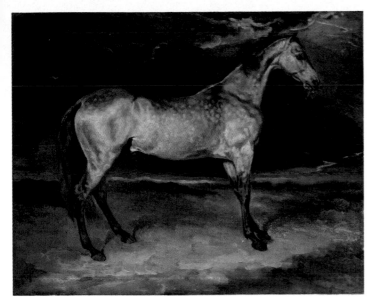

JEAN-LOUIS-ANDRÉ-THÉODORE
  GÉRICAULT
born Rouen 1791, died Paris 1824
A horse frightened by lightning 1813(?)
canvas 48.9 × 60.3
Purchased 1938

JEAN-BAPTISTE-CAMILLE COROT
born and died Paris, 1796–1875
Avignon from the west c 1836
canvas 33.7 × 73
signed
Bequeathed 1917

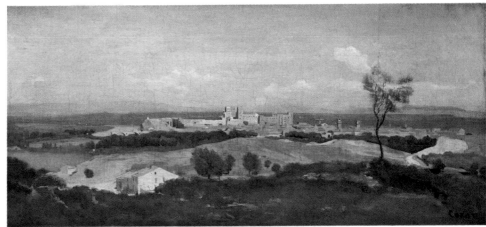

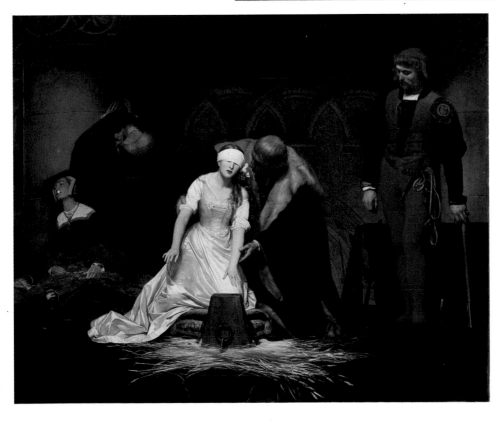

PAUL DELAROCHE
born and died Paris, 1795–1856
The execution of Lady Jane Grey 1833
canvas 246 × 297
signed and dated
Bequeathed 1902

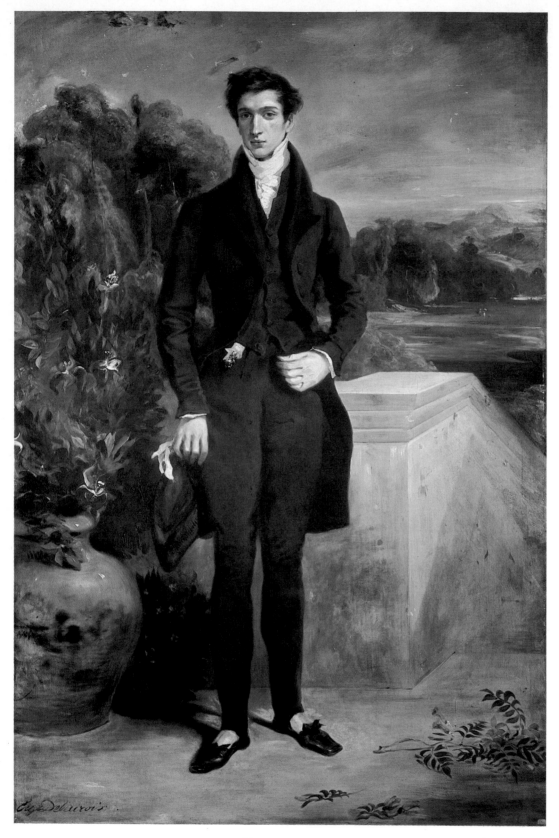

FERDINAND-VICTOR-EUGÈNE DELACROIX
born and died Paris, 1798–1863
Baron Schwiter 1826/30
canvas 218 × 143
signed
Purchased 1918

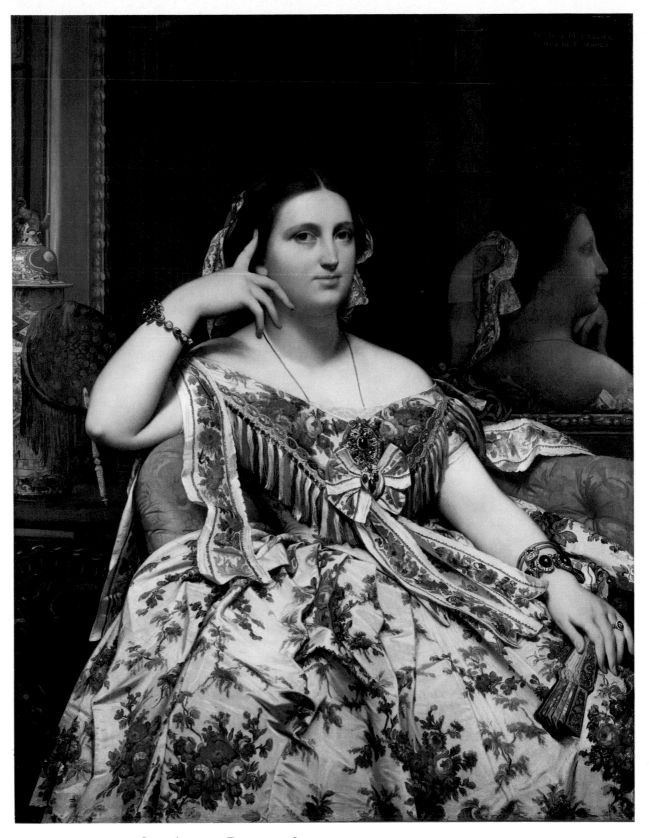

JEAN-AUGUSTE-DOMINIQUE INGRES
born Montauban 1780, died Paris 1867
Madame Moitessier seated 1856
canvas 120 × 92.1
Inscribed with the sitter's name
signed and dated
Purchased 1936

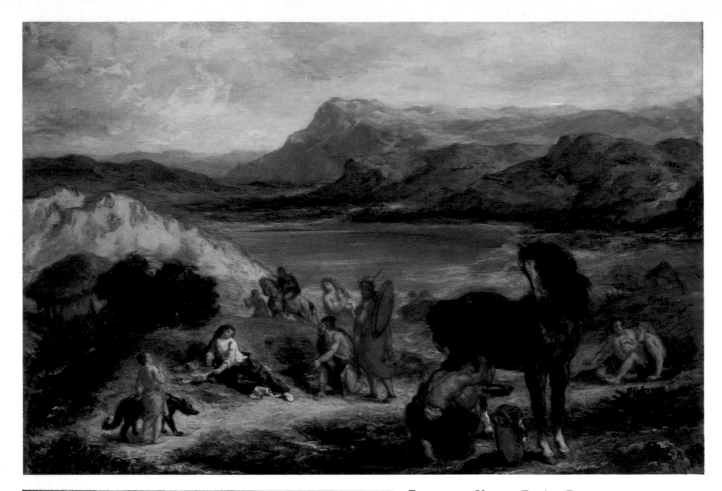

FERDINAND-VICTOR-EUGÈNE DELACROIX
born and died Paris, 1798–1863
Ovid among the Scythians 1859
canvas 87.6 × 130.2
signed and dated
Purchased 1956

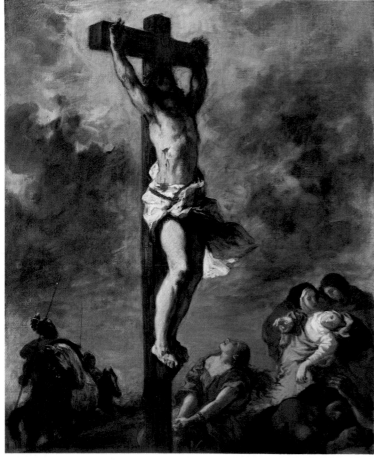

FERDINAND-VICTOR-EUGÈNE DELACROIX
born and died Paris, 1798–1863
Christ on the Cross 1853
canvas 73.3 × 59.5
signed and dated
Purchased 1976

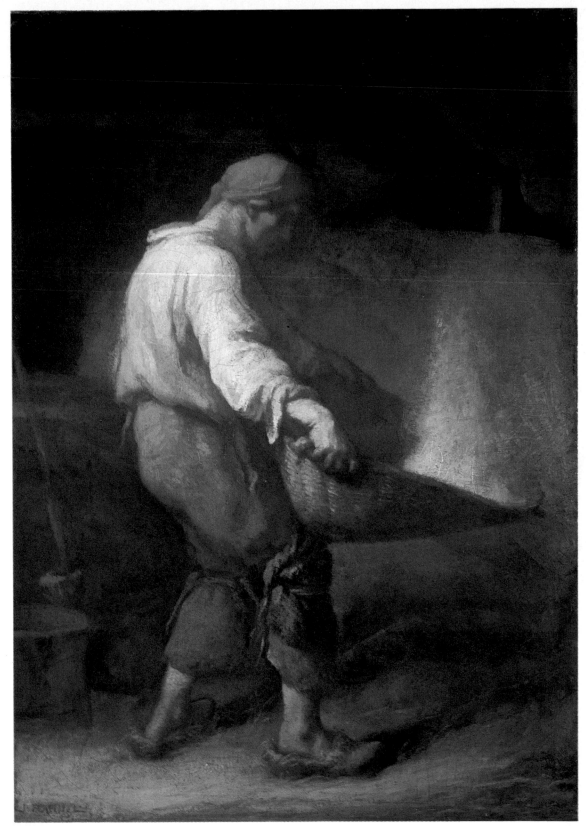

JEAN-FRANÇOIS MILLET
born Gruchy 1814, died Barbizon 1875
The winnower 1847/48
canvas 100 × 71
signed
Purchased 1978

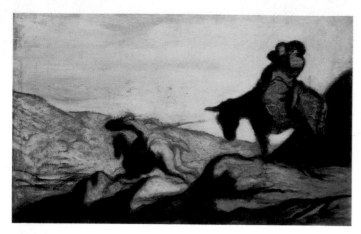

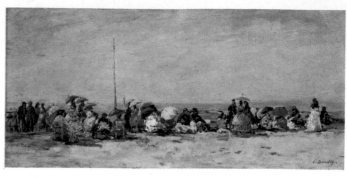

HONORÉ-VICTORIN DAUMIER
born Marseilles 1808, died Paris 1879
Don Quixote and Sancho Panza (unfinished)
wood 40.3 × 64.1
Bequeathed 1917

LOUIS-EUGÈNE BOUDIN
born Honfleur 1824, died Deauville 1898
Beach scene, Trouville 1860s
wood 21.6 × 45.8 signed
Bequeathed 1960

CLAUDE-OSCAR MONET
born Paris 1840, died Giverny 1926
Bathers at La Grenouillère 1869
canvas 73 × 92
signed and dated
Bequeathed 1979

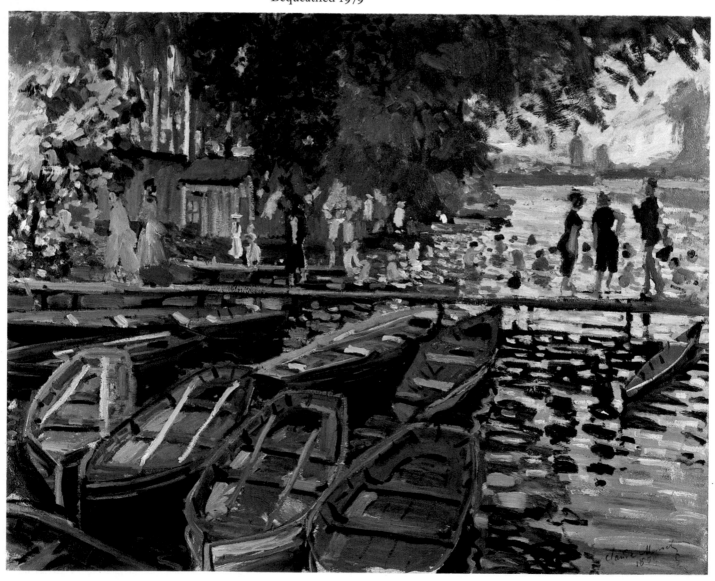

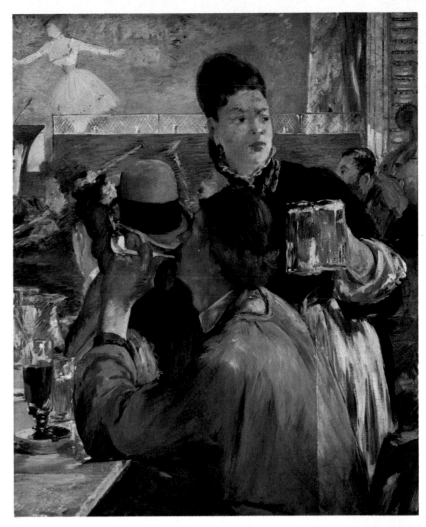

EDOUARD MANET
born and died Paris, 1832–1883
The waitress 1878/79
canvas 97.1 × 77.5
signed and dated
Presented 1924

EDOUARD MANET
born and died Paris, 1832–1883
Music in the Tuileries Gardens 1860/62
canvas 76.2 × 118.1
signed and dated
Bequeathed 1917

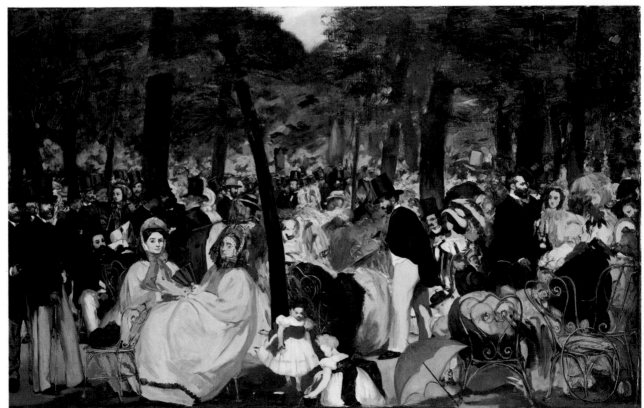

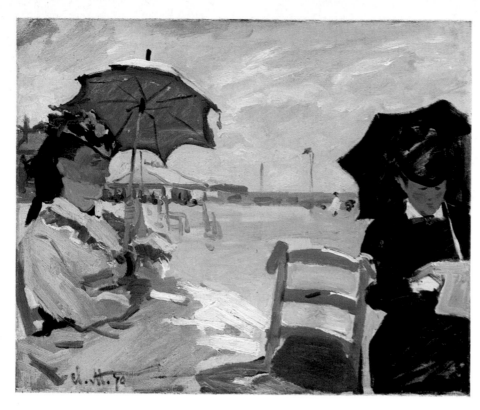

CLAUDE-OSCAR MONET
born Paris 1840, died Giverny 1926
The beach at Trouville 1870
canvas 37.5 × 45.7
signed and dated
Presented 1924

CAMILLE PISSARRO
born St. Thomas, Virgin Islands 1830,
  died Paris 1903
View from Louveciennes c 1870
canvas 52.5 × 82
signed
Bequeathed 1917

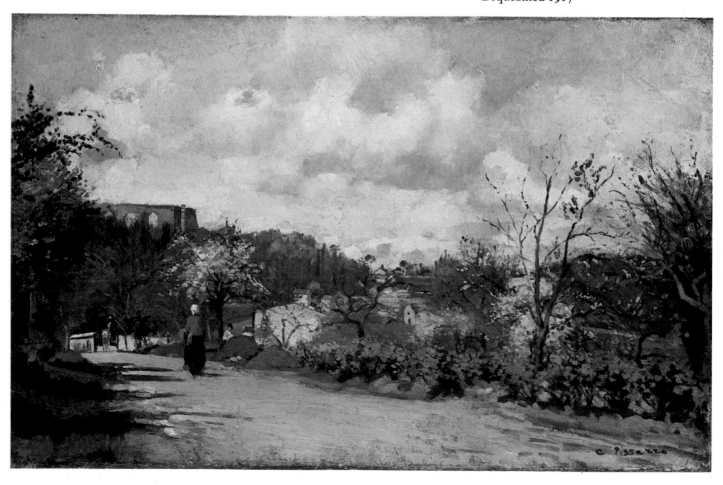

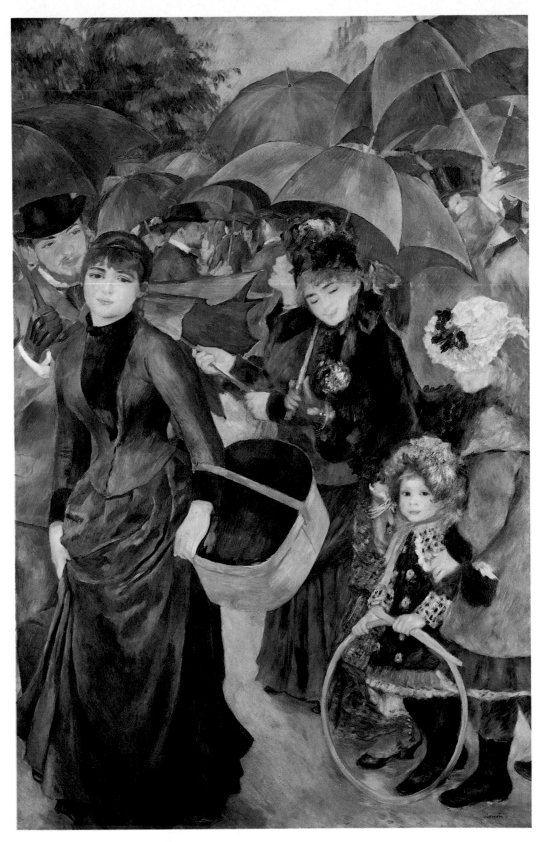

PIERRE-AUGUSTE RENOIR
born Limoges 1841, died Cagnes 1919
The umbrellas c 1880/85
canvas 180.3 × 114.9
signed
Bequeathed 1917

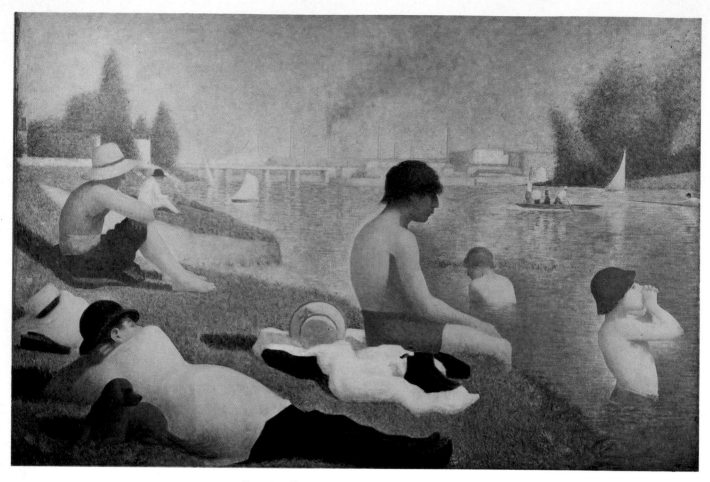

VINCENT VAN GOGH
born Groot-Zundert 1853, died
    Auvers-sur-Oise 1890
Sunflowers 1888
canvas 92 × 73 signed
Presented 1924

GEORGES-PIERRE SEURAT
born and died Paris, 1859–1891
Bathers, Asnières 1883/84
canvas 201 × 300
signed
Presented 1924

VINCENT VAN GOGH
born Groot-Zundert 1853, died Auvers-sur-
    Oise 1890
The chair and the pipe 1889
canvas 92 × 73
signed
Presented 1924

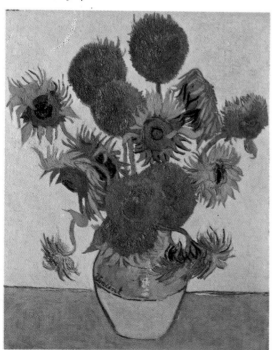

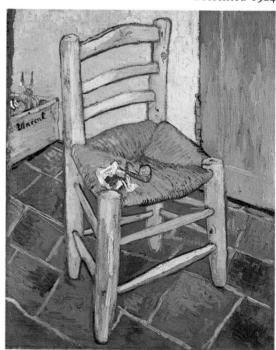

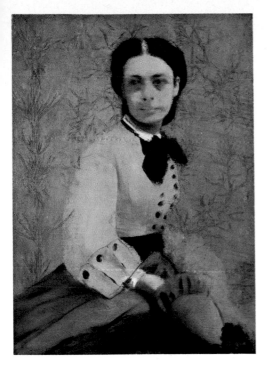

HILAIRE-GERMAIN-EDGAR DEGAS
born and died Paris, 1834–1917
Princess Metternich probably 1870
canvas 40.6 × 28.8
Presented 1918

HENRI DE TOULOUSE-LAUTREC
born Albi 1864, died Château de Malrome 1901
Woman seated in a garden 1891
millboard 66.7 × 52.8
Presented 1926

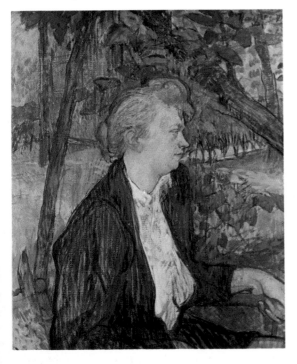

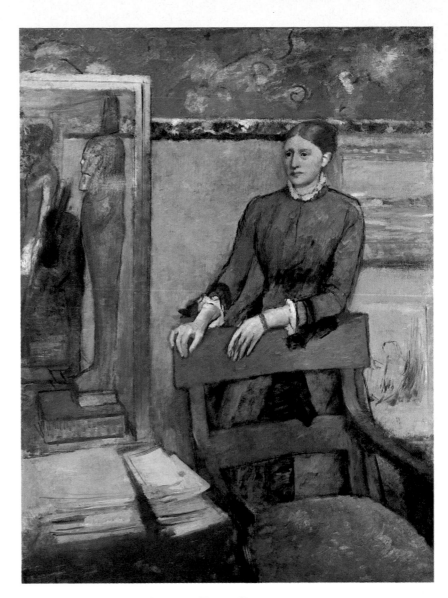

HILAIRE-GERMAIN-EDGAR DEGAS
born and died Paris, 1834–1917
Hélène Rouart in her father's study 1886
canvas 161 × 120
Purchased 1981

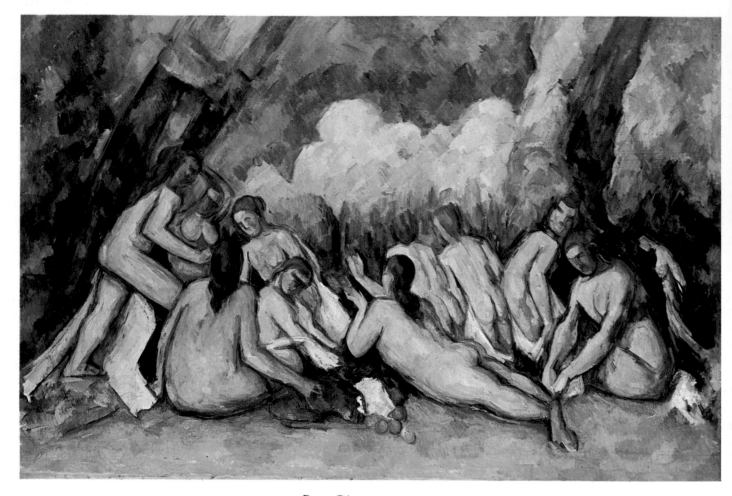

PAUL CÉZANNE
born and died Aix-en-Provence, 1839–1906
The large bathers c 1895/1904
canvas 127 × 196
Purchased 1964

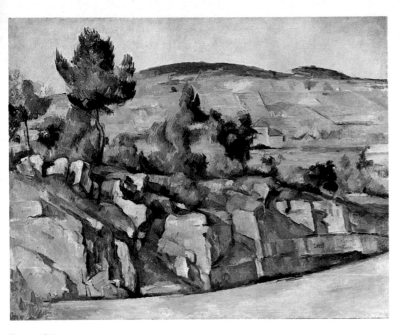

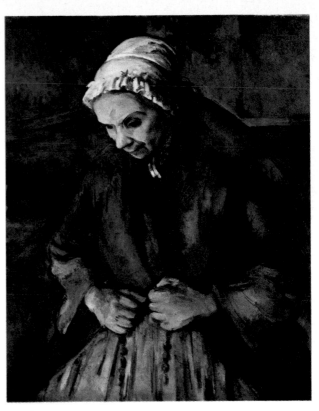

PAUL CÉZANNE
born and died Aix-en-Provence, 1839–1906
Mountains in Provence 1886/90
canvas 63.5 × 79.4
Purchased 1926

PAUL CÉZANNE
born and died Aix-en-Provence, 1839–1906
An old woman with a rosary 1896
canvas 80.6 × 65.5
Purchased 1953

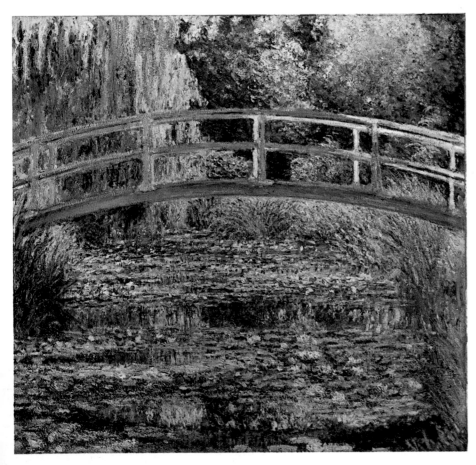

CLAUDE-OSCAR MONET
born Paris 1840, died Giverny 1926
The water-lily pond 1899
canvas 88.3 × 92.1
signed and dated
Purchased 1927

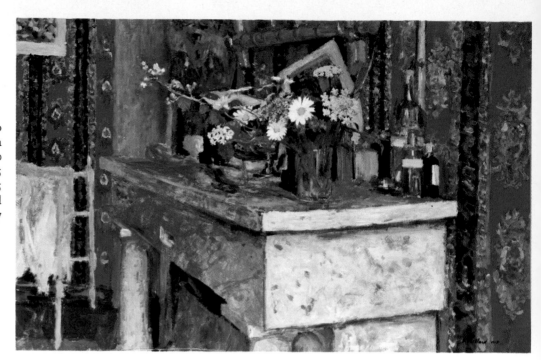

EDOUARD VUILLARD
born Cuiseaux 1868, died La
Baule 1940
The chimney-piece 1905
canvas 51.4 × 77.5
signed and dated
Purchased 1917

HENRI ROUSSEAU called 'LE
DOUANIER'
born Laval 1844, died Paris
1910
Tropical storm with a tiger 1891
canvas 129.8 × 161.9
signed and dated
Purchased 1972

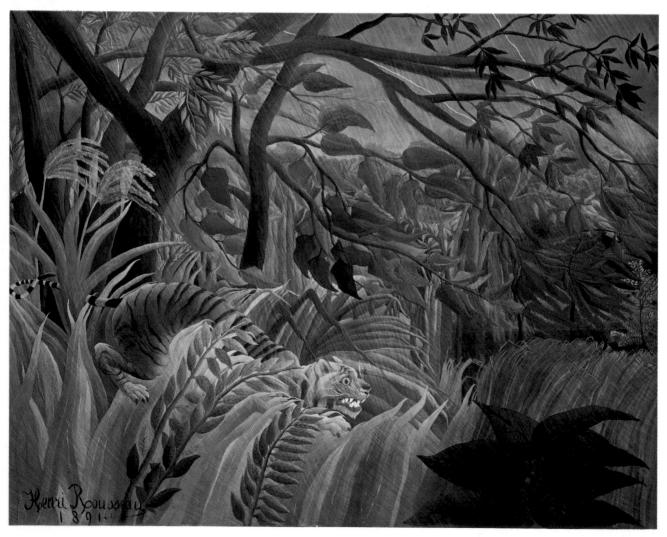

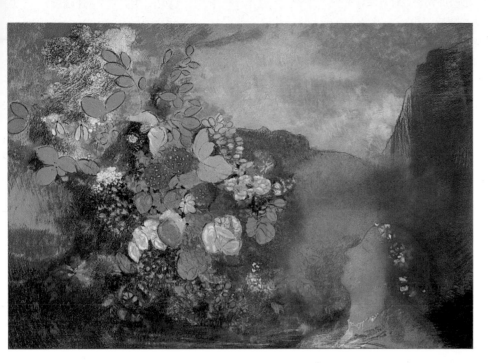

ODILON REDON
born Bordeaux 1840, died Paris 1916
Ophelia among the flowers c 1905/8
pastel 64 × 91
signed
Purchased 1977

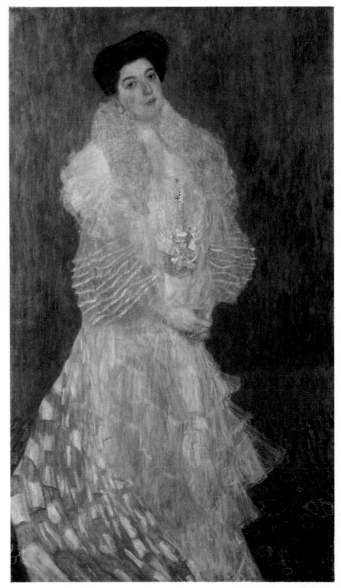

GUSTAV KLIMT
born and died Vienna, 1862–1918
Hermine Gallia 1904
canvas 170.5 × 96.5
signed
Purchased 1976

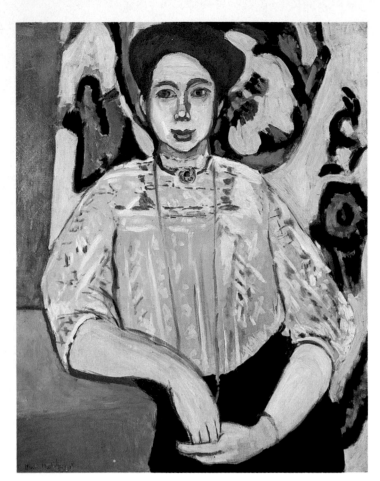

HENRI MATISSE
born Cateau-Cambrésis 1869, died Nice 1954
Portrait of Greta Moll 1908
canvas 92 × 73
signed and dated
Purchased 1979

PABLO RUIZ PICASSO
born Malaga 1881, died Mougins 1973
Bowl of fruit, bottle and violin 1914
canvas 92 × 73
signed
Purchased 1979

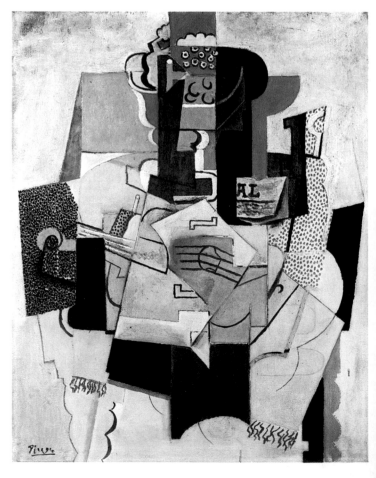

Index

Altdorfer, Albrecht, *Christ taking leave of His Mother*, 8, 30, 43

Angelico, Fra, 11; *Christ Glorified in the Court of Heaven*, 18

Angerstein, John Julius, 5, 11, 45, 46, 61, 85

Antonello da Messina, 29; *Portrait of a man*, 24; *St Jerome in his Study*, 24

Averkamp, Hendrick, *A winter scene with skaters near a castle*, 64

Baldovinetti, Alesso, *Portrait of a lady*, 19

Baldung, Hans, 29; *Portrait of a man*, 41

Barocci, Federico, *'La Madonna del Gatto'*, 45, 59

Barry, Edward, 7

Bartolommeo, Fra, 11

Bassano, Jacopo, *The Good Samaritan*, 59

Battoni, Pompeo Girolamo, *Time orders Old Age to destroy Beauty*, 105

Beaumont, Sir George, 5, 61, 85, 103

Bellini, Giovanni, *Madonna of the Meadow*, 11, 25, 29; *The Agony in the Garden*, 25; *The Doge Leonardo Loredan*, 25

Berchem, Nicolaes, 61; *A man and youth ploughing*, 62, 70

Borch, Gerard ter, *A woman making music with two men*, 73

Bosch, Hieronymus, *Christ mocked*, 39

Both, Jan, 61; *A rocky landscape with an ox-cart*, 70

Botticelli, Sandro, 11; *Venus and Mars*, 12, 27; *The Mystic Nativity*, 27; *Portrait of a young man*, 27; *Venus and Mars*, 27

Boucher, François, 85, 103; *Landscape with a watermill*, 114; *Pan and Syrinx*, 114

Boudin, Louis-Eugène, *Beach scene Trouville*, 132

Bouts, Dieric, *Entombment*, 36

Boxall, Sir William, 11, 45, 123

Bramantino, *The Adoration of the Kings*, 24

Bronzino, Angelo, *An allegory*, 46, 51

Bruegel, Pieter, the Elder, *The Adoration of the Kings*, 39

Brugghen, Hendrick ter, *Jacob reproaching Laban*, 64

Burton, Sir Frederick, 7, 11, 86, 123

Campin, Robert, 29; *The Virgin and Child before a firescreen*, 32; *A woman*, 32

Canaletto, 103; *'The stonemason's yard'*, 103, 107; *Venice: the basin of S. Marco on Ascension Day*, 107

Cappelle, Jan van de, 61; *A shipping scene with a Dutch yacht firing a salute*, 70

Caravaggio, 85; *Supper at Emmaus*, 85, 87

Carracci, Annibale, 11; *Christ appearing to St Peter on the Appian Way*, 85, 88; *'The Three Maries'*, 85, 89

Cezanne, Paul, 8; *The large bathers*, 138; *Mountains in Provence*, 139; *An old woman with a rosary*, 139

Champaigne, Philippe de, *Cardinal Richelieu*, 92

Chardin, Jean-Baptiste Siméon, *The young schoolmistress*, 113

Christus, Petrus, *Portrait of a young man*, 33

Cima da Conegliano, 11; *The Virgin and Child*, 26

Claude, Gellée, 5, 85, 86, 123; *The enchanted castle*, 8; *Cephalus and Procris*, 85, 97; *Hagar and the Angel*, 86, 95; *The embarkation of the Queen of Sheba*, 97

Constable, John, *The Haywain*, 86; *The cornfield*, 123; *Salisbury Cathedral*, 123, 126

Cornelis van Haarlem, *The preaching of St John the Baptist*, 63

Corot, Jean-Baptiste-Camille, 123; *Avignon from the west*, 123, 127

Correggio, Antonio, 11; *Madonna of the basket*, 45, 50; *Ecce Homo*, 45; *School of Love*, 45, 50

Courtauld, Samuel, 124

Costa, Lorenzo, *A concert*, 21

Cranach, Lucas, the Elder, *Cupid complaining to Venus*, 41

Crivelli, Carlo, 11; *The Annunciation with St Emidius*, 21

Cuyp, Albert, *Hilly river landscape*, 61, 71

Daubigny, Charles-François, 123

Daumier, Honoré-Victorin, *Don Quixote and Sancho Panza*, 132

David, Gerard, *The Adoration of the Kings*, 37; *The Virgin and Child with saints and donor*, 37

David, Jacques-Louis, 123

Degas, Hilaire-Germain-Edgar, 124; *Princess Metternich*, 137; *Hélène Rouart in her father's study*, 137

Delacroix, Ferdinand-Victor-Eugène, 123; *Baron Schwiter*, 124, 128; *Ovid among the Scythians*, 130; *Christ on the Cross*, 130

Delaroche, Paul, *The Execution of Lady Jane Grey*, 127

Detroy, Jean-François, *Jason swearing eternal affection to Medea*, 109

Domenichino, 85; *Landscape with Tobias and the Angel*, 85, 89

Dou, Gerrit, *A poulterer's shop*, 71

Drouais, François-Hubert, *Madame de Pompadour*, 104, 112–13

Duccio, 11, 124; *The Annunciation*, 13; *The Virgin and Child*, 14

Dughet, Gaspard, 86; *Ariccia*, 96

Dürer, Albrecht, 29, 30; *The painter's father*, 42

Dyck, Anthony van, 61; *Equestrian portrait of Charles I*, 61, 83; *Woman and Child*, 61, 81; *Lady Elizabeth Thimbleby and Dorothy, Viscountess Andover*, 61, 62

Eastlake, Sir Charles Lock, 7, 11, 12, 29, 45, 123

Elsheimer, Adam, 85; *Tobias and the Archangel Raphael*, 89

Eyck, Jan van, 29, 124; *Arnolfini Marriage*, 29, 34; *Man in a turban*, 29; *Portrait of a young man*, 33

Fabritius, Carel, *Self-portrait*, 69

Fragonard, Jean-Honoré, 8; *Psyche showing her sisters her gifts from Cupid*, 104, 111

Francia, Francesco, *The Virgin and Child with Saints*, 24

French School, *'The Wilton Diptych'*, 30, 31

Gainsborough, Thomas, *The Watering Place*, 61, 103, 117; *Mr and Mrs Andrews*, 103, 120; *The Morning Walk*, 103, 118

Gauguin, Paul, 124

Géricault, Jean-Louis-André-Théodore, *A horse frightened by lightning*, 127

Giordano, Luca, 85; *St Anthony of Padua*, 91

Giorgione, *'Il Tramonto'*, 55; *The Adoration of the Magi*, 55

Giovanni di Paolo, *The Baptism of Christ*, 15

Gogh, Vincent van, 124; *Sunflowers*, 136; *The chair and the pipe*, 136

Gossaert, Jan, see Mabuse

Goya, Francisco de, 104; *The Duke of Wellington*, 104, 122; *A scene from 'The Forcibly Bewitched'*, 122; *Doña Isabel de Porcel*, 122

Goyen, Jan van, *A view of Overschie*, 70

Greco, El, *Christ driving the traders from the Temple*, 86, 100; *The Adoration of the Name of Jesus*, 100

Guardi, Francesco, *A caprice with ruins on the seashore*, 108

Guercino, 85, *Incredulity of St Thomas*, 85, 90

Hals, Frans, *Portrait of a man*, 62, 65; *Young man holding a skull*, 62, 66

Heyden, Jan van der, 62; *An Architectural fantasy*, 73

Hobbema, Meyndert, 61; *The Avenue, Middelharnis*, 62, 76

Hogarth, William, *'Marriage à la Mode'*, 103; *The countess's morning levée*, 116

Holbein, Hans, the Younger, 29; *The Ambassadors*, 30, 44; *Christina of Denmark*, 30, 44

Holwell Carr, Rev, 5, 11, 45, 61, 85

Honthorst, Gerrit van, *Christ before the High Priest*, 63

Hoogh, Pieter de, *Interior*, 62; *The courtyard of a house*, 62, 75

Ingres, Jean-Auguste-Dominique, 123, 124; *Madame Moitessier seated*, 129

Jameson, Mrs Anne, 61

Jordaens, Jacob, *Govaert van Surpele and his wife*, 61, 84

Kalf, Willem, 8; *Still-life with the drinking-horn of the St Sebastian Archer's Guild, a lobster and glasses*, 77

Klimt, Gustav, 8, 124; *Hermine Gallia*, 141

Koninck, Philips, *Extensive landscape with a road by a ruin*, 71

Lancret, Nicolas, *The Ages of Man*, 103; *'La Tasse du Chocolat'*, 103, 114

Lane, Sir Hugh, 7, 123, 124

Lawrence, Sir Thomas, 6; *Queen Charlotte*, 104, 121

Lenain, Louis, *The Adoration of the Shepherds*, 93

Leonardo da Vinci, *The Virgin of the Rocks*, 45, 48; *The Virgin and Child with St Anne and St John the Baptist*, 45, 47

Lippi, Fra Filippo, *The Annunciation*, 18

Lippi, Filippino, *The Adoration of the Kings*, 28

Lochner, Stephen, 30; *St Matthew, St Catherine and St John the Evangelist*, 40

Longhi, Pietro, *A fortune-teller at Venice*, 108

Lotto, Lorenzo, *A lady as Lucretia*, 58

Lucas van Leyden, *A man aged thirty-eight*, 39

Mabuse, 29; *A little girl*, 38; *The Adoration of the Kings*, 38

Maes, Nicolaes, *Sleeping maid and her servant*, 72

Manet, Edouard, *Music in the Tuileries Gardens*, 123, 134; *The execution of the Emperor Maximilian*, 124; *The Waitress*, 124, 133

Mantegna, Andrea, 11, *Virgin and Child with the Magdalen and St John the Baptist*, 20; *Samson and Delilah*, 20; *The Agony in the Garden*, 23

Masaccio, *The Virgin and Child*, 12, 16

Masolino, ascribed to, *St John the Baptist and St Jerome*, 18

Master of Liesborn, 29; *The Annunciation*, 40

Master of the St Bartholomew Altarpiece, 29; *St Peter and St Dorothy*, 40

Matisse, Henri, 8; *Portrait of Greta Moll*, 124, 142

Memlinc, Hans, 29; *The Virgin and Child with saints and donors*, 35

Metsu, Gabriel, *Man and woman beside a virginal*, 62, 73

Michelangelo, 45, 86; *The Entombment*, 45, 52

Millet, Jean-François, *The Winnower*, 8, 124, 131

Monaco, Lorenzo, *Coronation of the Virgin*, 11, 14

Monet, Claude-Oscar, *Bathers at La Grenouillère*, 8, 132; *Beach at Trouville*, 124; *The Water-lily pond*, 139

Moreau, Gustave, 8, 124

Moretto da Brescia, *Portrait of a young man*, 58

Moroni, Giovanni Battista, *Portrait of a man, 'The Tailor'*, 58

Murillo, Bartolomé Esteban, *Peasant boy leaning on a sill*, 86, 99; *The Two Trinities*, 86, 102; *Self-portrait*, 99

National Art-Collections Fund, 8, 30, 86

Nattier, Jean-Marc, *Manon Balletti*, 109

Niccolo dell'Abate, attributed to, *The Story of Aristaeus*, 55

Oost, Jacob van, *A boy aged eleven*, 84

Orcagna, Style of, *Noli me tangere*, 14

Palma Vecchio, *Portrait of a poet, probably Ariosto*, 58

Parmigianino, *The Madonna and Child with St John the Baptist and St Jerome*, 45, 54; *The Mystic Marriage of St Catherine*, 54

Patenier, Joachim, *St Jerome in a rocky landscape*, 38

Peel, Sir Robert, 7, 11, 61

Perronneau, Jean-Baptiste, *Portrait of Jacques Cazotte*, 104, 115

Perugino, Pietro, 11, 12; *The Virgin and Child with St Raphael and St Michael*, 28

Picasso, Pablo, 8; *Bowl of Fruit, bottle and violin*, 124, 142

Piero della Francesca, 11; *The Nativity*, 20; *The Baptism of Christ*, 22

Piero di Cosimo, 12; *A mythological subject*, 28
Pisanello, 30; *The Vision of St Eustace*, 15
Pissarro, Camille, *View from Louveciennes*, 123, 134
Pittoni, Giovanni Battista, *The Nativity with God the Father and the Holy Ghost*, 105
Pollaiuolo, Antonio and Piero del, 11; The *Martyrdom of St Sebastian*, 12, 19
Pontormo, *Joseph in Egypt*, 54
Poussin, Nicolas, 85, 86; *Adoration of the Golden Calf*, 86, 96; *A Bacchanalian Revel*, 93; *Landscape with a man killed by a snake*, 93; *Adoration of the Shepherds*, 94

Raphael, 45; *The Ansidei Madonna*, 45, 49; *Pope Julius II*, 46, 47; *St Catherine of Alexandria*, 47
Redon, Odilon, 8, 124; *Ophelia among the flowers*, 141
Rembrandt van Rijn, 5, 61; *Hendrickje Stoffels*, 8, 62, 67; *Woman bathing in a stream*, 61, 65; *Belshazzar's Feast*, 62, 69; *Jacob Trip*, 62; *Margaretha de Geer*, 62, 68; *Self-portrait aged sixty-three*, 65
Reni, Guido, *Susannah and the Elders*, 11; *Lot and his daughters*, 85, 90
Renoir, Pierre-Auguste, *The umbrellas*, 123, 135
Reynolds, Sir Joshua, *Lord Heathfield*, 103, *General Sir Banastre Tarleton*, 104, 119; *Anne, Countess of Albemarle*, 104, 120
Ribera, Jusepe de, 85; *Jacob with the flock of Laban*, 102
Ricci, Sebastiano, *Bacchus and Ariadne*, 105
Rigaud, Hyacinthe, *Portrait of Antoine Paris*, 104, 109
Rosa, Salvator, 86; *Landscape with Tobias and the Angel*, 91
Rousseau, Henri, 8, 123, 124; *Tropical storm with a tiger*, 140

Rubens, Peeter Pauwel, 5, 61; *Peace and War*, 6, 61, 78; *Samson and Delilah*, 8, 61, 79; *Autumn landscape*, 61, 80; *'Le Chapeau de Paille'*, 62, 82; *The Judgement of Paris*, 80
Ruisdael, Jacob van, 61; *Landscape with a ruined castle and a church*, 62, 76
Ruskin, John, 8, 11

Saenredam, Pieter, *The Grote Kerk, Haarlem*, 62, 69
Salting, George, 7, 62, 123
Sarto, Andrea del, *Portrait of a young man*, 50
Sassetta, *The whim of the young St Francis to become a soldier*, 15
Sebastiano del Piombo, *The Raising of Lazarus*, 45, 46, 52–3
Seurat, Georges-Pierre, *Bathers, Asnières*, 124, 136
Signorelli, Luca, *Adoration of the Shepherds*, 26
Spranger, Bartholomeus, *The Adoration of the Kings*, 41
Steen, Jan, 62; *The effects of intemperance*, 72
Strozzi, Bernardo, *Personification of Fame*, 91
Stubbs, George, *The Milbanke and Melbourne families*, 104, 116

Taylor, Sir John, 7
Thoré, Theophile, 62
Tiepolo, Giambattista, 103; *An allegory with Venus and Time*, 103, 106; *The banquet of Cleopatra*, 108
Tiepolo, Giovanni Domenico, *The procession of the Trojan Horse into Troy*, 108
Tintoretto, Jacopo, 86; *The Origin of the Milky Way*, 59; *St George and the Dragon*, 45, 60
Titian, *Bacchus and Ariadne*, 6, 11, 45, 46, 56, 86; *Holy Family*, 45; *The death of Actaeon*, 46, 57; *Portrait of a man*, 57, 62; *Noli me tangere*, 57

Toulouse-Lautrec, Henri de, *Woman seated in a garden*, 137
Tura, Cosimo, *St Jerome*, 21
Turner, Joseph Mallord William, 123; *The 'Fighting Téméraire'*, 123, 125; *Rain, steam and speed*, 123, 126; *Dido building Carthage*, 123

Uccello, Paolo, *Battle of San Romano*, 11, 17, 30

Valentin, Le, *The Four Ages of Man*, 85, 90
Veláquez, Diego, 46; *Kitchen scene with Christ in the house of Martha and Mary*, 85, 98; *The Boar Hunt*, 86; *Philip IV of Spain in brown and silver*, 86, 101; *'The Rokeby Venus'*, 86, 98
Velde, Willem van de, 62
Vermeer, Johannes, *Young woman seated at a virginal*, 62, 73; *Young woman standing at a virginal*, 62, 74
Vernet, Claude-Joseph, *A sea-shore*, 115
Veronese, Paolo, 45; *Family of Darius before Alexander*, 45, 60; *The Vision of St Helena*, 60
Verrocchio, Andrea del, 11
Verrocchio, follower of, *Tobias and the Angel*, 26
Vouet, Simon, *Ceres and harvesting Cupids*, 92
Vuillard, Edouard, *The chimney-piece*, 140

Watteau, Jean-Antoine, 103; *'La Gamme d'Amour'*, 103, 110
Weyden, Rogier van der, 29; *Pietà*, 36; *St Ivo*, 36
Wilkins, William, 5–6
Wilson, Richard, *Holt Bridge on the River Dee*, 117
'Wilton Diptych', See French School
Wynn Ellis, 7, 62

Zoffany, Johann, *Mrs Oswald*, 121
Zurburan, Francisco de, *St Margaret*, 102